Runn

My Journe
Forgiveness and Faithfulness
By John M. Chilson

MW01291043

This book is a series of "snapshots" I wrote to help me better understand my journey to find and run with God. I hope it will help you better understand your journey.

"A series of whimsical, thoughtful reflections on life and faith. Each story is a jumping–off point for deeper personal reflection. It's the kind of book you can use once a day or from time to time. A good addition to your devotional practices!"

Pastor Cris Crisfield
Rocky Mountain Christian Church
Niwot, CO

"This book is easy to read, but it will help you see your relationship with God and with other people in new ways. With plenty of wisdom and thought–provoking questions, it's a good study for individuals or couples and even for small groups. You'll enjoy this one!"

Richard Cox
Church Small Group Leader
Longmont, CO

"A fun and thought provoking read. I found myself convicted with a loving approach. Healing medicine without the bitter after taste."

R.A. Easter
Former Youth Pastor
Greeley, CO

RUNNING WITH GOD

My Journey to Find
God's Love,
Forgiveness and
Faithfulness

John M. Chilson

1st Printing

ISBN-13: 978-1467963480
ISBN-10: 1467963488

**Dedicated to my mother,
Jean Lynn Chilson Brader,**
whose unfailing cheerful faith in a very
personal and loving God encouraged me
and helped my own faith to grow.

**And to my father,
John Albert Chilson,**
whose view that theology should be simple, easily
understood and easily explained helped keep me
focused on what I believe is the good news of the
Gospel message.

A special "Thank You" to Deloris Giltner
who edited this book and my three previous
books. She has been a great teacher, a gentle
mentor, a very dear friend and she
has almost broken me of using passive verbs.

A special "Thank You" to all who read early drafts,
gave me their input and supported me with their
prayers. I especially appreciate the help I received
from my wife Darlene, my son Paul and his wife
Kari, Richard Cox, Cris Crisfield, R.A. Easter, my
son's partner Karen Kavnar, Mary Ann Louis and
Lee Quaintance. They gave me their time, insights
and guidance — even when we disagreed. This
book is better because of them.

Any errors of spelling, punctuation,
grammar, theology or anything else
are purely mine and, when found,
will be corrected in a future edition.

Running With God

Contents

Forward..1

Running With God 3

A Dangerous Song.................................7

Awe.. 12

Big Is Easy, Small Is Hard........................... 15

What's My Attitude? 18

Trust..22

Crooked Lines 25

Holding God's Hand 29

Dangerous People 33

Do I Have To Share? 38

What Is Faith?...41

Do I Covet Your Blessings? 48

My Friend.. 51

The God Scale...54

The Greatest Passion.............................. 58

I'm Depressed 61

Sing Hallelujah On Good Friday? 67

Thank You 71

Not In The Mood......................................74

Heaven 78

The Weaver 82

Contents

Anticipation 86

Things Change 90

Love! That's All 94

Pain And Comfort 98

Santa Wouldn't Do That 101

Worry or Pray? 105

A Smaller Cross 108

Shaken Or Stirred? 112

They Call Me Grandpa 118

Thoughts On A Mountain Stream 124

Trials And Tribulations 128

Choices... 133

In Bondage To Sin 136

Made In God's Image.............................. 140

What's Next For Me? 147

What's Next For You? 151

About The Author 163

Bible Verses 164

Sources 166

Running With God

Favorite Pages

_____

_____

_____

_____

_____

_____

_____

_____

_____

_____

_____

_____

_____

_____

_____

_____

_____

_____

_____

_____

_____

_____

Forward

Every once in a while it seems God gives me a sharp nudge in the ribs with His elbow and says something like, "Did you see that? That is just a small part of who I am."

Some of these "elbow nudges from God" come from various books I read. Others come in the middle of the night when I can't sleep and still others catch me unawares when I least expect them.

None of them are spiritually or theologically profound. That's because my father always told me, religion and faith should be kept simple enough for a child to understand.

Now let me share with you an unexpected discovery. When I had written down a number of these "elbow nudges" I looked at them for the first time as a group and not just as individual thoughts. It was then I discovered a common theme running through them:

God seems to be saying, "Trust Me, grab hold of My hand and run with Me. And don't forget to laugh while we do it."

You see, I believe life is a journey, the greatest of adventures. Life is to be enjoyed and savored — like the taste of cold, creamy home-made ice cream on a hot July day; like a warm, blazing fireplace and a good book on a cold winter day; like the taste of Grandma Leatha's (my mother-in-law) cinnamon rolls fresh from the oven or like a hug and a kiss from my wife, my children or my grandchildren.

Running With God

This book is a series of "snapshots" of my journey with God showing some of the "nudges" I've received along the way.

By the way, as you read this book, I hope you don't think that I never suffer from depression, sin, envy or any other weakness.

BECAUSE I DO!

That's why I wrote down these thoughts in the first place — to help *me* trust and love God more. It was only much later that I realized they might also help someone else. My prayer is that this book will help you too in some small way.

The questions after each chapter are in the first person "I" because I want you, the reader, to ask the questions of yourself. You don't need to know how I would answer them because what is important is how you answer them.

As you read this book I hope you will use the blank lines to record your own "nudges from God".

> Lord Jesus, I thank You for allowing me to share Your love and forgiveness and faithfulness with the readers of this book. Amen.

Running With God

"I want to walk with Jesus."

"I want Jesus to walk with me."

There are many prayers, songs and books about *walking* with Jesus.

Well, I want to *RUN* with Jesus.

Several times in my life God has moved very quickly to make significant changes. I remember clearly the spring of 1976. I had a good job and a lovely home in Iowa. My wife and our three young children were happily settled. We had just purchased a new car.

One day I prayed what I later realized was a *very* dangerous prayer, "God, if You want to change anything in my life You will have to do it. Otherwise, I am not going to change anything."

Running With God

Only a few short months later we sold our lovely home and our new car. We shipped a few of our belongings and put the rest in long–term storage. My wife and I and our three children moved to a small town west of London, England where I had a new job working for an American marketing company.

This move significantly changed the life of each member of our family — for the better.

- My wife and I were baptized a year later in the small Baptist church in Henley–On–Thames, England.
- We started learning to walk closer with God, relying on Him every day.
- Our children discovered it is fun to make new friends and experience new cultures.

WOW! When God gets ready to run, hang on tight!

Jesus said we should always be ready to run with Him...

Be dressed for service and keep your lamps burning, as though you were waiting for your master to return from the wedding feast. Then you will be ready to open the door and let him in the moment he arrives and knocks.

Luke 12:35–36 NLT

Dear Lord, help me always be prepared, always ready, always willing to run with You wherever You wish to take me. And please help me focus my life on holding tight to Your hand. Amen

Running With God

Let's think about running with God...

1. Have I ever experienced God working quickly in my life?
2. What was the situation and what was the outcome?
3. What can I do to help me focus on holding onto God's hand?

_____

_____

_____

_____

_____

_____

_____

_____

_____

_____

_____

_____

_____

_____

_____

_____

A Dangerous Song

Have Thine own way, Lord!

Have Thine own way!

Thou art the Potter, I am the clay.

Mold me and make me after Thy will,

While I am waiting, yielded and still.

By Adelaide A. Pollard [1]

How glibly I sing this and other songs like it. Often I don't really think about the words. But, if God is the potter and I am the clay, then God can make me into anything He wants. Right?

Of course, I like to think of Him making me into a beautiful cup or some other fine piece of art or, at least, a vase to hold beautiful flowers.

But what if God needs a chamber pot? (If you don't know what a chamber pot is, ask the oldest person you know to explain it to you.)

Running With God

Am I really willing to take abuse without reward, work in filth and stench just because God wants me to?

Yet, that is just what Mother Theresa did. Over the years, others, too numerous to count, have done it too. They loved the unlovable, lived an unthinkably low life and dedicated their lives to living for others.

Why?
For love?
Whose love?
God's love!

The Apostle Paul said something similar in his letter to the Christians in Rome...

> **Should the thing that was created say to the one who created it, "Why have you made me like this?" When a potter makes jars out of clay, doesn't he have a right to use the same lump of clay to make one jar for decoration and another to throw garbage into?**
>
> Romans 9:20b–21 NLT

A Dangerous Song

Matthew, one of Jesus' disciples, recorded His words about taking care of others...

Then these righteous ones will reply, "Lord, when did we ever see you hungry and feed you? Or thirsty and give you something to drink? Or a stranger and show you hospitality? Or naked and give you clothing? When did we ever see you sick or in prison and visit you?"

And the King will say, "I tell you the truth, when you did it to one of the least of these my brothers and sisters, you were doing it to me!"
Matthew 25:37–40 NLT

Lord, please forgive me for all the times I sang "Have thine own way, Lord," without really thinking about what the words meant. Now that I have thought about them, I'm scared. I don't know if I can really pray this prayer.

I'm scared of what this prayer might do to my life, my family, my job, my home. But, Lord, I trust You and I love You. So, with a deep sense of nervousness, I do pray to You...

Lord, I am willing to be made willing. That's all I can do now. The rest is up to You.

Amen.

Let's think about letting God be in charge...

1. If I sing the words of this song and REALLY mean them, what does that mean?
2. Can the words of this song change my life?
3. How?
4. Can I ever sing the words of this song and REALLY mean them?
5. Now?
   If not now, why not and when?

_____

_____

_____

_____

_____

_____

_____

_____

_____

_____

_____

Awe

Have you ever met a truly important person? Perhaps it was the owner of a large company, maybe it was a very wealthy person or even a movie star or an important political person.

How did you feel and react? I must confess that I am often a little (well, maybe, a lot) in awe of such people.

However, on a few rare occasions when they were with their children, I saw this "important" person in a totally different light.

Children are almost never in awe of a parent. Maybe it is because they see their parents in so many different situations and know them for who they really are. I sometimes wish I could be part of that "important" person's close family and learn to know them without any sense of awe.

Over the years I worshipped in many churches of many different denominations. In some God was described as a pal, my buddy, someone I could hang out with. In others He was proclaimed to be holier than holy, higher than high, untouchable and unknowable.

It is very easy to become confused. Is this the same God? I don't see how He can be high and holy in one church and my buddy in another.

Can I ever know Him without a tremendous sense of awe?

Yes, praise God, I can.

Why?

How?

Because I am now one of God's children.

The Apostle Paul wrote to the Christian's in Rome about being one of God's children...

For all who are led by the Spirit of God are children of God. So you have not received a spirit that makes you fearful slaves. Instead, you received God's Spirit when he adopted you as his own children. Now we call him, "Abba, Father." For his Spirit joins with our spirit to affirm that we are God's children.
Romans 8:14–16 NLT

Thank You Heavenly Father for making me one of Your children. Help me retain a sense of awe at Your high holiness; and yet, feel free to approach You with open arms, as a child to a father. Amen.

Let's think about being in awe...

Who can I name that puts me in awe?

1. What is it about them that does that?
2. If I spent a lot of time with them, would I still be in awe?
3. Am I in awe of God?
4. If I spent more time with Him, would I still be in awe?

_____

_____

_____

_____

_____

_____

_____

_____

_____

_____

_____

_____

_____

_____

_____

Big Is Easy, Small Is Hard

In the Old Testament story from the book of 2nd Kings, Naaman, commander of the army of the King of Aram, was trying to get rid of his leprosy. Elisha, God's Prophet, told him to go wash himself — a small thing. So small that Naaman didn't want to do it. But when he finally did, WOW!!! What a blessing. If you haven't read the whole story lately, look it up — 2nd Kings Chapter 5. It's a neat story. Share it with your children.

Anyway, I often have the same problem myself — Lord, ask me to do something BIG FOR YOU and I will give it my best shot.

What?

- God, You just want me to phone someone and say "hello"?
- God, You just want me to pop in and visit someone for five minutes?
- God, You just want me to mention my own problem as a prayer request in front of everyone in church?
- God, You just want me to attend a short committee meeting once a month?
- God, You just want me to do what???

Sorry, God, don't have time, too busy, won't work, too embarrassing, I don't know them well enough, they might not like it.

Boy, oh boy, can I ever come up with the excuses.

But once in a while I actually do what I'm asked. I do my small task and that's the end of it. Sometimes I find out later that my small task was a huge blessing to someone, way out of proportion to my small effort. Then I really feel foolish for dragging my feet.

Maybe next time I won't drag them quite so much.

Here's the *small* thing Elisha told the king to do ...

Elisha sent a messenger out to him with this message: "Go and wash yourself seven times in the Jordan River. Then your skin will be restored, and you will be healed of your leprosy."

2nd Kings 5:10 NLT

Lord, if You have a small task for me to do, please don't give me any peace until I do it. In the meantime, draw me closer until all I can see is You. Amen.

Let's think about doing things for God...

1. Can I remember small things I've done that brought unexpectedly big blessings to someone else?

2. Can I remember big things I've done that brought unexpectedly small blessings and very little thanks?

3. Which do I prefer doing for God — big things or little things? Why?

_____

_____

_____

_____

_____

_____

_____

_____

_____

_____

_____

_____

What's My Attitude?

Charles Swindoll[12], Christian pastor, author, speaker and founder of Insight For Living said this about attitude...

> The longer I live, the more I realize the impact of attitude on life. Attitude, to me, is more important than facts.
>
> It is more important than the past, than education, than money, than circumstances, than failures, than successes, than what other people think or say or do.
>
> It is more important than appearance, giftedness or skill.
>
> It will make or break a company, a church, a home.
>
> The remarkable thing is we have a choice every day regarding the attitude we will embrace for that day. We cannot change the past. We cannot change the fact that people will act in a certain way. We cannot change the inevitable. The only thing we can do is play on the one string we have, and that is our attitude.

What's My Attitude?

> I am convinced that life is 10% what happens to me and 90% how I react to it. And so it is with you.
>
> We are in charge of our ATTITUDES.

At one time I had a group of teenagers working for me. Often it was their first job. I would tell them over and over, "A good attitude will cover a multitude of mistakes."

I would rather work with someone who has a great attitude and makes mistakes than work with someone who is perfect but has a poor attitude. Wouldn't you?

The Apostle Paul said this about attitude...

For the Kingdom of God is not a matter of what we eat or drink, but of living a life of goodness and peace and joy in the Holy Spirit. If you serve Christ with this attitude, you will please God. And other people will approve of you, too.
Romans 14:17–18 NLT

Do everything without complaining and arguing, so that no one can criticize you.
Philippians 2:14–15a NLT

Father in Heaven, give me today my daily bread and let my attitude show everyone how grateful I am. Amen.

What's My Attitude?

Let's think about attitude...

1. What has my attitude been lately?
2. Have I upset anyone because of my attitude?
3. Is my attitude one that encourages others to talk with me and do things with me or does my attitude push them away?
4. What might happen if, for a week, I showed a smile on my face and displayed a willing, helpful attitude?
5. How would such a week affect me?
6. How would such a week affect my family, my friends, my co–workers, my church?

_____

_____

_____

_____

_____

_____

_____

_____

_____

_____

_____

Trust

We once owned a Scots Terrier named Heidi. She was a delightful little dog with a large, fierce heart. She loved to chase our sons and nip at their ankles when they played kick–ball in the back yard. Although we had plans of raising puppies, Heidi had a health problem and the vet encouraged us to have her spayed. So we did.

One morning I took up Heidi's food and water bowls so that she couldn't eat or drink. Later I took her to a strange place, the vet's office, and left her with strangers. During the day, although they used an anesthetic, they caused her some pain. Later that day I picked her up and took her home. Eventually she healed and her life moved on.

Now, there was no way short of Heaven that I could explain to Heidi that what I did was necessary for her own health and well–being. Yet, although I had been the cause of her pain, that lovely little dog never ceased to love and trust me.

I am convinced that there are things that happen in my life that I won't understand until I talk with God at a later time. Therefore, I need to continue trusting Him.

For many years I had a little note from a long–ago worship service. Until it fell apart, I kept that wrinkled note stuck to my bathroom mirror...

> MY FATHER, I DO NOT UNDERSTAND THEE
> BUT I TRUST THEE.

John, one of Jesus' disciples, recorded His words about trust...

Don't let your hearts be troubled. Trust in God, and trust also in me.
John 14:1 NLT

James, another of Jesus' disciples, wrote this about being testing and trusting...

Dear brothers and sisters, when troubles come your way, consider it an opportunity for great joy. For you know that when your faith is tested, your endurance has a chance to grow. So let it grow, for when your endurance is fully developed, you will be perfect and complete, needing nothing.
James 1:2–4 NLT

Lord, I ask for strong, unbreakable trust in You. Please help me go through my daily difficulties and troubles trusting completely in You. Amen.

Let's think about trust...

1. Can I remember a time when something unplanned and unwanted happened to me?
2. How did that make me feel?
3. How did I respond?
4. How did my response affect others around me at the time?
5. If God is truly in control, how should I respond when something unplanned or unwanted happens?

_____

_____

_____

_____

_____

_____

_____

_____

_____

_____

_____

_____

Crooked Lines

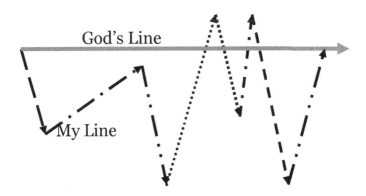

There is an old proverb, not Biblical but perhaps Irish, that says, "God draws straight with crooked lines."

Boy is that ever true.

Looking backward over my life I see many of the bends in the line from where I started until where I am now.

Looking forward, however, all I can see is a short straight line because I can only see as far as the next bend in the line.

A good example of God drawing straight with crooked lines is my son, Paul, and the children's Christian picture book he wrote and published…

- **1st Part of the Line:** Paul wrote a poem to help his three small children understand God's love. He titled the poem, "The Love That Is True."

- **2nd Part:** Paul sent a copy of his poem to a Christian friend in Russia. The friend wrote back that he liked the poem and that it should be in a book with pictures. The friend, a professional film animator, offered to draw the pictures.
- **3rd Part:** The pictures provided by Paul's friend were stunningly beautiful.
- **4th Part:** Paul learned about book design and book printing.
- **5th Part:** Paul and his wife formed a small publishing company.
- **6th Part:** Paul had 3,000 books printed and stored in his basement.
- **7th Part:** Paul and his wife learned how to market the book and how to deliver the copies to the buyers.
- **8th Part:** Paul's book will be in 300 Christian book stores for Christmas 2011.
- **9th Part:** Paul is developing as a public speaker in order to share his book with children and parents.
- **10th Part:** Sorry, there is a bend in the line and we can't see past it — yet.

Do you see the pattern? Paul and I have talked about this several times. If, when he first thought about writing the poem, he had seen the complete line stretched out *straight* in front of him, he might never have taken the first step and written the poem.

Looking backward over my life, I see similar patterns of crooked lines. If I had seen the complete straight line going into the far distant future, very probably I would *never* have taken the first step.

God's crooked lines are meant to lead us to Heaven. If I could see the lines my life will follow, all the way from birth to Heaven, it would scare me so much I wouldn't be able to take one step.

Jesus is the only person who saw God's complete plan for His life stretched out before Him as a straight line. Read Matthew 26:36–43 to see how difficult this made life for Him.

The Apostle Paul wrote to the Christians in Corinth about not seeing clearly...

> **Now we see things imperfectly as in a cloudy mirror, but then we will see everything with perfect clarity. All that I know now is partial and incomplete, but then I will know everything completely, just as God now knows me completely.**
>
> 1st Corinthians 13:12 NLT

Loving Father, help me realize that I do not need to see or understand Your complete plan. Help me be ready to take the next step as You lead me, hanging tightly to Your hand. Amen

Let's think about God's crooked lines...

1. Can I look back and see God's crooked lines in my life?

2. Can I think of a situation in my life where I would not have taken the first step if I'd seen the entire path?

3. Can I think of an opportunity I did not take because the first step was too big, too scary or too difficult?

4. Could God be calling me now to take that first step?

5. If so, what should I do?

_____

_____

_____

_____

_____

_____

_____

_____

_____

_____

_____

_____

Holding God's Hand

I spend a lot of time running from God and then running back to God and then running from God and then... and then...

You get the picture.

But shouldn't I be running **with** God **and** holding onto His hand?

I enjoy walking or running hand–in–hand with someone. It is very comforting because I know I am less likely to fall and less likely to get lost when I hold someone's hand and they hold mine.

I wonder what life would be like if every day I held onto God's hand, holding His promises and love in my heart.

The thing is, God's hand is always there, always ready for me to grab hold.

So why don't I grab His hand?

Fear?

Lack of trust?

"I can do it myself; I want to do it my way."

Darn, that just sort–of slipped out. Did I really write that?

Well, I guess I've finally found the core of my problem — I'd rather do it myself, even if it means walking in fear, than walk with God without fear.

Why?

Well, I really hate to admit it but it's because I'm not sure I always want to go where God wants to lead me or do what God wants me to do.

- I really do want to take that exciting new job, even though it means more time away from my wife, my children and my church.
- I really don't want to visit my elderly neighbor today.
- I really don't want to actively participate or speak up in the adult Sunday school class I attend.
- I really don't want to say something when the people I work with swear or cuss or cheat the company.
- I really don't want to be "un–cool" by telling my children they shouldn't be doing what all their friends are doing.
- I really don't want to play catch and talk with my son right now, maybe later.

Oops!

Didn't I recently sing, "Have thine own way, Lord"?

God's word says we should trust Him and not be afraid...

> **Trust in the LORD with all your heart; do not depend on your own understanding. Seek his will in all you do, and he will show you which path to take.**
>
> Proverbs 3:5–6 NLT

> **You need not be afraid of sudden disaster or the destruction that comes upon the wicked, for the LORD is your security. He will keep your foot from being caught in a trap.**
>
> Proverbs 3:24–26 NLT

Okay, Lord, I admit it. I often act like a small child, wanting to do everything myself, in my way, in my time. Why do You continue to put up with me? Oh, because of Your Son?

Okay God, I'll try harder. But like everything else, I need trust and faith to come from You because I really don't have any of my own. Amen

Running With God

Let's think about holding God's hand...

1. Do I even know if I'm holding God's hand or not?
   How do I know?

2. Down deep, what is really keeping me from running hand–in–hand with God?

3. What can I do to overcome my reluctance to holding God's hand and running with Him?
   Is it something I can do?
   Is it something God can do?

_____

_____

_____

_____

_____

_____

_____

_____

_____

_____

_____

_____

Dangerous People

Who would have thought that a baby born in a stable could grow up to be such a dangerous person? He actually believed He was the Son of God. But He didn't act like it. How ridiculous can you get?

Suppose I believed that I was a prince, the son of a king, and acted like it. I would strut around in fine clothes, expecting everyone to bow down before me, expecting everyone to serve my every whim and throwing a royal tantrum when I didn't get it. That's what I would do. Wouldn't you?

But Jesus didn't act like that. He called the religious leaders bad names, ate many of His meals with prostitutes and tax collectors, associated with losers and low life of all kinds. Worse, He touched them — with His own hands. He even washed the feet of His followers. How gross is that?

It wouldn't be so bad if Jesus was the only one that acted that way, but stories have been told over the last 2,000 years of other people behaving almost like He did. These other people believed that Jesus really was the Son of God. I'm sure you've heard some of those stories...

- The story about a man called Francis of Assisi
- Another story about a German named Martin Luther
- A story about someone named Martin Luther King, Jr.

- One about some guy called Albert Schweitzer
- Even a story about a woman referred to simply as Mother Theresa
- Add John Newton to the list — he wrote "Amazing Grace"

The stories of people like this seem to go on and on forever throughout history.

What was with these people? They seemed totally fearless. They acted like they were on a mission to save the world, or at least a small part of it. Many of them gave up the comforts of a good job, warm home and loving family.

Didn't they get it?

That's not how real people are supposed to act. Or are they?

Look at the results. Of the six people listed above...

- Three received the Nobel Peace Prize
- One has an entire group of Christians named after him (the Lutherans)
- One has a U.S. holiday in his honor
- One wrote a song just about everyone knows how to sing
- One is already called and another is being considered, of all things, a Saint.

What's with these people? What did they know that you and I don't know?

Some of these people I've mentioned had some questionable doings in their life. Some of them fought periods of deep depression. Many of them had continuing questions about what they were doing.

But history doesn't dwell much on their human failings. Instead we hear about their devotion to Jesus and their love of mankind.

Dangerous people!

People **transformed** by God's Holy Spirit.

What would happen if I became transformed like they were?

What would happen if you and I both were transformed like they were?

What would happen if everyone was transformed like they were?

It might just turn the world upside down — or right–side up.

It could be the end of the world as we know it.

Hmmmm!

Maybe that wouldn't be so bad.

John, one of Jesus' disciples, recorded what Jesus said that made those people so dangerous...

This is my commandment: Love each other in the same way I have loved you. There is no greater love than to lay down one's life for one's friends.

You are my friends if you do what I command. I no longer call you slaves, because a master doesn't confide in his slaves. Now you are my friends, since I have told you everything the Father told me.

You didn't choose me. I chose you. I appointed you to go and produce lasting fruit, so that the Father will give you whatever you ask for, using my name. This is my command: Love each other.

This is my command: Love each other. If the world hates you, remember that it hated me first. The world would love you as one of its own if you belonged to it, but you are no longer part of the world. I chose you to come out of the world, so it hates you.

Do you remember what I told you? "A slave is not greater than the master." Since they persecuted me, naturally they will persecute you. And if they had listened to me, they would listen to you. They will do all this to you because of me, for they have rejected the One who sent me.

John 15:12–21 NLT

Lord God, Father of my Lord, Jesus Christ, change me that I might love others completely and unconditionally, remembering it is not my will, but Yours, O God. Amen.

Let's think about being a dangerous person...

1. Why was Jesus so dangerous?
2. Why were the people listed above so dangerous?
3. Who do I know that is dangerous in the same way?
4. Is one of them my pastor?
5. Am I dangerous in the same way as the people listed in this chapter?
6. Could I be?
7. Should I be?
8. Am I willing to let God transform me? Now?
   If not now, why not and when?

_____

_____

_____

_____

_____

_____

_____

_____

_____

Do I Have To Share?

If I have a full pie, of course I'll share a piece with someone else.

If I have two cars, I'll loan one to a friend — the oldest car, of course.

If I have $200 in my pocket, of course I'll give $1 or $2, maybe even $5 or $10, to someone who has none.

The problem is that it's really hard for me to be generous when there is only one piece of my favorite pie and someone else also wants it.

It is hard for me to be generous when I have a new car, all bright and shiny and running good and someone without a car needs to borrow it.

It is hard for me to be generous when I only have $5.00 in my pocket and someone without any money asks me for help.

It's even harder when I only have $25 in my billfold, very little in my checking account and utility bills a month past due and then my church asks for a donation. What should I give them?

And yet, being generous when it is NOT easy is exactly what God asks me to do.

It all comes back to trust.

If I can trust God, then I can be a better steward and I can be more generous.

After all, if I have already turned everything over to God, it is not really my pie, my car or my money anyway.

Right?

Two lessons from God's word...

John (the Baptist) replied, "If you have two shirts, give one to the poor. If you have food, share it with those who are hungry."

Luke 3:11 NLT

All the believers were united in heart and mind. And they felt that what they owned was not their own, so they shared everything they had.

Acts 4:32 NLT

Lord, help me trust more in You and become more generous with my time, my money, my everything. Amen.

Let's think about sharing...

1. Can I remember a situation where I felt pressure to give something away but I resisted?
2. Why did I resist?
3. What did I end up doing and how did I feel afterwards?
4. Can I remember a situation where I spontaneously gave something to someone?
5. How did I feel when I did that?
6. Did that gift cost me anything?

_____

_____

_____

_____

_____

_____

_____

_____

_____

_____

_____

_____

What Is Faith?

All my life both my father and I were often puzzled and surprised by my mother's actions.

Mom would just jump right in to help someone even if others might think her help wasn't completely appropriate. She often told me, "Well, I got myself into another mess but the Lord will take care of it."

Minutes before my mother's funeral the minister received a phone call from a woman in another state who wanted to share her story about my mother. She told the minister that one morning, my mother (who then lived just down the street) knocked on her door.

Mom simply said that for several years she had been going regularly to Bible Study Fellowship, a Bible study group. Since my mother had completed the study course she told her neighbor she was volunteering to watch her small children one morning a week so that she could attend the Bible study.

What is interesting is that my mother and her neighbor didn't know each other very well and had never before discussed attending a Bible study. However, the result of this conversation was that for several years this woman was able to attend the Bible study knowing her children were well cared for by my mother.

It was only when I stumbled onto this writing by Martin Luther that I finally began to understand my mother.

Martin Luther's Definition of Faith [2]

Faith is not what some people think it is. Their human dream is a delusion. Because they observe that faith is not followed by good works or a better life, they fall into error, even though they speak and hear much about faith.

"Faith is not enough," they say, "You must do good works, you must be pious to be saved." They think that, when you hear the gospel, you start working, creating by your own strength a thankful heart which says, "I believe."

That is what they think true faith is. But, because this is a human idea, a dream, the heart never learns anything from it, so it does nothing and reform doesn't come from this "faith," either.

Instead, faith is God's work in us that changes us and gives new birth from God. It kills the Old Adam and makes us completely different people.

It changes our hearts, our spirits, our thoughts and all our powers. It brings the Holy Spirit with it. Yes, it is a living, creative, active and powerful thing, this faith.

Faith cannot help doing good works constantly. It doesn't stop to ask if good works ought to be done, but before anyone asks, it already has done them and continues to do them without ceasing.

Anyone who does not do good works in this manner is an unbeliever. He stumbles around and looks for faith and good works, even though he does not know what faith or good works are. Yet he gossips and chatters about faith and good works with many words.

Faith is a living, bold trust in God's grace, so certain of God's favor that it would risk death a thousand times trusting in it. Such confidence and knowledge of God's grace makes you happy, joyful and bold in your relationship to God and all creatures.

The Holy Spirit makes this happen through faith. Because of it, you freely, willingly and joyfully do good to everyone, serve everyone, suffer all kinds of things, love and praise the God who has shown you such grace. Thus, it is just as impossible to separate faith and works as it is to separate heat and light from fire!

Therefore, watch out for your own false ideas and guard against good–for–nothing gossips, who think they're smart enough to define faith and works, but really are the greatest of fools. Ask God to work faith in you, or you will remain forever without faith, no matter what you wish, say or can do.

The Apostle Paul described faith this way to the early Christians...

Faith is the confidence that what we hope for will actually happen; it gives us assurance about things we cannot see.

Hebrews 11:1 NLT

What Is Faith?

Here is what the Apostle James said of faith...

What good is it, dear brothers and sisters, if you say you have faith but don't show it by your actions? Can that kind of faith save anyone? Suppose you see a brother or sister who has no food or clothing, and you say, "Good-bye and have a good day; stay warm and eat well" — but then you don't give that person any food or clothing. What good does that do?

So you see, faith by itself isn't enough. Unless it produces good deeds, it is dead and useless.

Now someone may argue, "Some people have faith; others have good deeds." But I say, "How can you show me your faith if you don't have good deeds? I will show you my faith by my good deeds."

You say you have faith, for you believe that there is one God. Good for you! Even the demons believe this, and they tremble in terror. How foolish! Can't you see that faith without good deeds is useless?

James 2:14–20 NLT

Running With God

Lord, send Your Holy Spirit to create such a faith in me that I will run boldly forward, holding your hand and doing Your will, wherever You take me. Amen.

Let's think about faith...

1. How have I been defining faith?
2. Does my definition match the Bible's definition or Martin Luther's definition?
3. If not, which definition do I think is correct and why?
4. What needs to be changed in me so that I can live with and practice God's definition of faith?
5. Am I willing to ask God to make that change in me?
6. Now?
   If not now, why not and when?

_____

_____

_____

_____

_____

_____

_____

_____

_____

_____

_____

Do I Covet Your Blessings?

For a while we had two large dogs living at our house — Clancy our aged Golden Retriever and Freeway our son's Great Dane/Boxer mix.

Because of Clancy's age, our vet suggested we encourage him to eat more by giving him some canned dog food along with his dry dog food. Well, that certainly worked great. He loved it.

And so did Freeway who quickly gained 10 pounds he didn't need.

As a result, while I gave Clancy a half a can of dog food, I started giving Freeway only one or two tablespoons, just enough so he wouldn't feel completely left out.

Freeway quickly realized what was happening. From then on, as soon as I opened a can of dog food, Freeway was immediately at my elbow, quietly begging for a larger portion. But I never gave it to him. He didn't need it and in the long run it would have been bad for him.

Oops!

I realized then how often I am just like Freeway. I see the apparently larger and greater blessings given to other people and I immediately beg God to give me some too. Let's face it, I'm just plain jealous.

I don't stop to think that maybe I don't need the greater blessings, that such blessings might, in the long run, be bad for me and that I have other blessings that may be even better if I'd simply stop to appreciate them properly.

Do I Covet Your Blessings?

The Tenth Commandment says...

"You must not covet your neighbor's house. You must not covet your neighbor's wife, male or female servant, ox or donkey, or anything else that belongs to your neighbor."

Exodus 20:17 NLT

Doesn't that also include my neighbor's blessings?

Lord, please help me be content with the blessings You give me. They are more than I can count. I thank You for them and I also give You thanks for my neighbor's blessings. Lord help me trust in Your wisdom to decide which blessings each of us truly needs. Amen.

Let's think about my blessings...

1. Have I ever desired a specific blessing only to later discover that I am better off without it?

2. Have I ever wished I could have some of the blessings that someone else is receiving?
Why?

3. How did it make me feel?
Who is the one making me feel that way?
Myself?

4. Has anyone ever expressed a desire to receive some of *my* blessings?
How did that make me feel?
How did I respond?

5. Why do I think "Thou shall not covet" is one of the Ten Commandments? Isn't coveting relatively harmless? What can coveting lead to?

My Friend

Several years ago there was a popular Christian song "You Are Jesus to Me." Well, I am very fortunate. I had a dear friend who was Jesus to me. He was patient with me, forgave my every harsh, unkind word or action and was always there for me — day or night.

When I couldn't sleep at night and I sat in the living room at three in the morning, he would get up from his warm bed and join me — without comment, complaint or criticism.

When I returned from a trip — short or long — he immediately was there to joyfully greet me, showing his great delight at my safe return home. When I ignored him, he continued to love me, hoping that I would notice him again soon.

Through his unceasing and unconditional love, he showed me that I, too, could love others, be patient with them and be faithful to them. Most important is how he reminded me of what an amazing, wonderful, loving friend I have in Jesus.

By the way, what was my friend's name?

His name was Clancy. He was a Golden Retriever and I *know* he will be waiting to greet me when I get to Heaven.

John, a disciple of Jesus, described Christian love this way...

Dear children, let's not merely say that we love each other; let us show the truth by our actions.
1st John 3:18 NLT

Dear Jesus, thank You for being my wonderful, constant friend. You are a friend to whom I can turn for help any time of day or night, with any problem or difficulty, for myself, my family, my friends, my church, for anyone.

Please help me be a patient, forgiving and faithful friend to others. And, dear Lord, please don't give up on me when I fail. Amen.

Let's think about being a friend...

1. Am I a best friend to anyone?
2. Is it necessary for the other person to think of me as their best friend?
3. What is keeping me from being a best friend to more people?
4. What would happen if I loved other people the way my dog loves me?

The God Scale

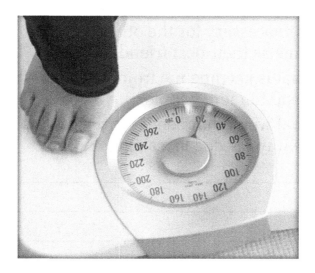

Some mornings as I get up, just before I take my shower, I find my way to the bathroom scales. I step on them and look to see the morning's verdict — up a little, up a lot or, "Praise God," no change from yesterday or, perhaps, maybe down a little.

You see, I'm overweight. Not a lot, at least by my reckoning, but enough that I can't just go and eat anything and everything. Darn. I sure do love good food.

Anyway, as I was contemplating the day's verdict from the scales, I thought, "Wouldn't it be neat to have a 'Near To God' scale?" I could step on it and it would tell me how near to God I am today.

Yeah, that would be neat, all right. But then I realized that such a scale would need only two markings on it — **FAR AWAY** and **VERY NEAR**.

And once it changed from **FAR AWAY** to **VERY NEAR**, the scale would be forever stuck on **VERY NEAR**.

Why?

Because God says that once we become one of His children, we are ALWAYS one of His children.

Once we are near to God, we are always near to Him, even when we don't feel like it, even when we don't feel He is near to us.

Now isn't that neat?

The Old Testament makes this point about God being near...

> **...the LORD our God is near to us whenever we call on him.**
> Deuteronomy 4:7b NLT

John, a disciple of Jesus, wrote about being a child of God in one of his letters...

> **But to all who believed him and accepted him, he gave the right to become children of God. They are reborn — not with a physical birth resulting from human passion or plan, but a birth that comes from God.**
> John 1:12–13 NLT

Dear Father God, I thank You that I am one of Your children and that when I feel far away from You, it is only my feelings and not reality because You really are *always* very, very near to me.

Help me, Father, to live my life today in full realization of the freedom and love that is mine because I am Your child. Amen.

Let's think about being near to God...

1. When was the last time I felt that God and I were far apart?

2. What was happening in my life at that time to make me feel that way?

3. How did I get over that *feeling* (if I ever did)?

4. Can that feeling of being far from God *ever* be true?
   Can that feeling *ever* be trusted?

5. If I know that feelings cannot be trusted, how will my life change?

_____

_____

_____

_____

_____

_____

_____

_____

_____

_____

_____

The Greatest Passion

During Lent, the six weeks leading up to Easter, we often speak of "The Passion" when referring to the crucifixion of Jesus.

However, as a father watching three children, and now 10 grandchildren, grow up, I have come to realize that the greatest passion of all was **NOT** the passion of Christ dying on the cross.

The greatest passion was the passion of the Father — the Father who loved us so much He sent His only Son to be crucified on a cross for my sins and for your sins.

I cannot imagine a love in which I would send my own child to die for someone else. I can hardly begin to understand such depth of unconditional love.

The only answer that makes any sense to me is that God deeply and passionately loves me, you and each one of us.

John, a disciple of Jesus, recorded what Jesus said about God's love for us...

For God loved the world so much that he gave his one and only Son, so that everyone who believes in him will not perish but have eternal life.

John 3:16 NLT

And Paul, a follower of Jesus, wrote this in one of his letters...

But God showed his great love for us by sending Christ to die for us while we were still sinners.

Romans 5:8 NLT

Father God, such love as Yours is too much for me, a sinner, to comprehend. I stand in awe within Your love and say that I am not worthy of such love.

I confess that I have not loved You with my whole heart or my neighbors as myself.

Create in me a pure heart, O God, and renew a steadfast spirit within me. Restore to me the joy of Your salvation and grant me a willing spirit to sustain me. Amen.

Let's think about love and sacrifice...

1. If my child died saving the life of a neighbor how would I feel?
2. Would I feel the same way if my child died fighting in a war to help people I don't know?
3. Is there a difference?
4. What is the difference?
5. Can I even imagine a situation where I would purposely send my child to die for someone I have never met?

_____

_____

_____

_____

_____

_____

_____

_____

_____

_____

_____

_____

I'm Depressed

It's ten o'clock at night. The house is all quiet. My dog is in his bed fast asleep. And I'm depressed. I have been for several weeks.

To make things worse, I just re–read some of the chapters I'm writing for this book and all that did was make me feel guilty:

- Guilty that I'm not seeing the banquet God has set before me ("Things Change," page 18)
- Guilty that I'm not more trusting of God ("Trust," page 22)
- Guilty that I'm not in the mood to serve God ("Not In The Mood," page 74)

The list goes on and on and I'm tired of feeling guilty and I'm tired of not being able to get out of my depression.

I'm tired of being tired.

And I really don't want to talk about it.

At the same time God seems to be saying to me, "Right now it's okay that you can't do these things. I understand. Really! For a season you are going through a tough time. You can do it, just continue to hang in there, continue to trust in Me and stop feeling guilty.

"Remember, I LOVE YOU! You are MY child and I am watching over you and I never sleep or go on vacation so I am always here for you."

Along with that thought, two of my chapters came to mind — "Trials And Tribulations," page 128 and "Pain And Comfort," page 98. Maybe there is a reason for this season. Maybe God can use it somehow.

I'm also reminded of "The Preacher" who in the book of Ecclesiastes, Chapter 3 talks about the seasons of life.

> **For everything there is a season,**
> **A time for every activity under**
> **heaven.**
> **A time to be born and a time to die.**
> **A time to plant and a time to**
> **harvest.**
>
> **A time to kill and a time to heal.**
> **A time to tear down**
> **and a time to build up.**
> **A time to cry and a time to laugh.**
> **A time to grieve and a time to**
> **dance.**
>
> **A time to scatter stones**
> **and a time to gather stones.**
> **A time to embrace**
> **and a time to turn away.**
> **A time to search**
> **and a time to quit searching.**
> **A time to keep and a time to throw**
> **away.**
>
> **A time to tear and a time to mend.**
> **A time to be quiet and a time to**
> **speak.**
> **A time to love and a time to hate.**
> **A time for war and a time for peace.**
>
> Ecclesiastes 3:1–8 NLT

I guess right now I'm in a time of grieving, crying and searching. But I need to remember it's only for a time.

Personal Note: I really did not want to write this chapter, especially now late at night. But I knew that if I didn't write it now it might never be written. Further, I believe there is someone else out there who is hurting as much or more than I am. If that person is you or someone you love and care about then I have several suggestions. I pray you will take them seriously.

First of all, phone someone — a pastor, friend, relative, co–worker, neighbor. Right now! Even if it is ten o'clock at night or three in the morning, if they are a friend and you tell them you need their help, they won't mind. Talk to them and ask them to pray with you. Set a time to meet with them personally to talk — today or tomorrow.

Secondly, make an appointment to see your doctor — soon. Sometimes depression can be caused by or made worse by a chemical imbalance. This can often be helped with medications or a change in your eating habits. But, the point is, seek your doctor's help now!

Finally, if the pain of your depression is so bad you can't live with it anymore, then drive or have someone else drive you or call a taxi or call 911 and go to the nearest hospital Emergency Room. There is help available. **Don't leave the hospital until you get it.** Treat this as you would a stroke or heart attack — critically important.

Go Now!

Running With God

God's word gives us this encouragement...

Have you never heard? Have you never understood? The LORD is the everlasting God, the Creator of all the earth. He never grows weak or weary. No one can measure the depths of his understanding.

He gives power to the weak and strength to the powerless. Even youths will become weak and tired, and young men will fall in exhaustion.

But those who trust in the LORD will find new strength. They will soar high on wings like eagles. They will run and not grow weary. They will walk and not faint.
Isaiah 40:28–31 NLT

"For I know the plans I have for you," says the LORD. "They are plans for good and not for disaster, to give you a future and a hope."
Jeremiah 29:11 NLT

Heavenly Father, I really don't know how to pray right now so I'll try to trust that You see and feel my pain and that You continue to love me, even though I don't feel very loved. Dear Jesus, stay close and hold my hand and walk with me during this terrible season of my life. Amen.

Let's consider depression a little more...

1. Have I ever been depressed?
2. Am I depressed right now?
3. Have I been depressed for more than a week?
4. If so, what can I do to get some help?
5. Can I start now?
   If not now, why not and when?

_____

_____

_____

_____

_____

_____

_____

_____

_____

_____

_____

_____

_____

_____

_____

Sing Hallelujah On Good Friday?

Many churches do not sing "Hallelujah" during Lent, especially not on Good Friday, the day we remember the crucifixion of Jesus. Lent is to be a season of rededication and repentance. Singing "Hallelujah" is saved for Easter morning.

In the song "Lord of The Dance" [3] one of the lines is "It's hard to dance with the devil on your back."

It's also hard to sing "Hallelujah" with the devil on your back.

It is hard to sing anything when my life is going to pieces...

- My hopes and dreams are in ruins
- My child, spouse, parent, friend or pet dies
- I lose my job, my home, my retirement savings

Unfortunately, the list of things that can go to pieces, and do, seems endless.

And yet, there are many places in the Bible, both the Old and New Testaments, that tell me to praise the Lord for all things and at all times.

Did Mary the mother of Jesus praise God when she stood at the foot of the Cross on Good Friday?

So let me ask, "How do I sing 'Hallelujah' on Good Friday?"

The only answer I have is "Any way I can."

And often with a sob in my voice and tears running down my face.

Encouragement comes from King David's poems...

I will praise the LORD at all times. I will constantly speak his praises.

Psalm 34:1 NLT

In my desperation I prayed, and the LORD listened; he saved me from all my troubles.

Psalm 34:6 NLT
I recommend reading the entire Psalm 34

Paul, a follower of Jesus, wrote these words in a letter to other Christians...

Can anything ever separate us from Christ's love? Does it mean he no longer loves us if we have trouble or calamity, or are persecuted, or hungry, or destitute, or in danger, or threatened with death? (As the Scriptures say, "For your sake we are killed every day; we are being slaughtered like sheep.")

No, despite all these things, overwhelming victory is ours through Christ, who loved us.

Sing Hallelujah On Good Friday?

**And I am convinced that nothing
can ever separate us from God's
love. Neither death nor life, neither
angels nor demons, neither our
fears for today nor our worries
about tomorrow — not even the
powers of hell can separate us from
God's love.**

**No power in the sky above or in the
earth below — indeed, nothing in all
creation will ever be able to
separate us from the love of God
that is revealed in Christ Jesus our
Lord.**

Romans 8:35-39 NLT

*Heavenly Father, please help me
sing "Hallelujah" to You even in the
worst times. Amen.*

Running With God

Let's think about singing Hallelujah...

1. When is the last time I sang "Hallelujah?"
2. Was it a happy time or a difficult time?
3. Can I list the top three difficulties I am going through right now?
4. Can I still sing "Hallelujah?"
5. How?

_____

_____

_____

_____

_____

_____

_____

_____

_____

_____

_____

_____

_____

_____

Thank You

Well, somebody around here should learn how to say "Thank you."

After all the work I did the least they could say is "Thank you."

Doesn't anyone ever get any appreciation around here?

How come **they** were thanked and I wasn't?

When I do something I want to be, no, I expect to be, appreciated and thanked.

RIGHT NOW!

Oops.

Sorry, Lord, I forgot my place. For a moment I thought I was the master but I am really only a servant.

Was it only last Sunday that I prayed and sang, "Take my life and use it any way that serves You"?

Guess I forgot these words of Jesus recorded by Luke...

> **And does the master thank the servant for doing what he was told to do? Of course not. In the same way, when you obey me you should say, "We are unworthy servants who have simply done our duty."**
>
> Luke 17:9–10 NLT

Paul, a follower of Christ, wrote this in a letter...

> **Work willingly at whatever you do, as though you were working for the Lord rather than for people. Remember that the Lord will give you an inheritance as your reward, and that the Master you are serving is Christ.**
>
> Colossians 3:23–24 NLT

Lord Jesus, You are King of my life. Let Your presence in my life be all the thanks I ever need or desire. Amen.

Let's think about being thanked...

1. How do I feel when my work at the church goes unrecognized?

2. Am I more likely to do some work just because it needs doing and I can do it or because someone will thank me for doing it?

3. Can I think of work that has been done but I don't know who did it?

4. When was the last time I did a significant amount of work without being recognized as the person who did it?

5. How did that make me feel and what did I do about it?

_____

_____

_____

_____

_____

_____

_____

_____

_____

_____

Not In The Mood

In the book "Dune" by Frank Herbert[4], the young prince Leto is told by his fighting instructor to get ready for a practice session. And Leto declines saying, "I'm not in the mood."

Oops! Wrong response.

The instructor yells back something like "Not in the mood? Being in the mood is for singing songs or romance, not for fighting."

Aren't these verses saying the same thing today to each of us? The Apostle Peter said...

And if someone asks about your Christian hope, always be ready to explain it.
1st Peter 3:15b NLT

And the Apostle Paul said...

Preach the word of God. Be prepared, whether the time is favorable or not.
2nd Timothy 4:2a NLT

I hate it when the Bible says things like that because I know it is talking directly to me...

I'm tired; I don't want to write Advent devotions right now. But they are needed for the church bulletin.

I'm busy and I don't want to take time now to talk to my friend or neighbor or co–worker or spouse or child or parent or stranger about God and Jesus and what my faith means to me. I'm not in the mood.

"Well, tough," Paul says.
"You're in God's Army now."
"Stop your complaining!
Start soldiering, soldier!"
YES, SIR!

Paul, a follower of Jesus, explained how to prepare...

Be strong in the Lord and in his mighty power. Put on all of God's armor SO that you will be able to stand firm against all strategies of the devil.

For we are not fighting against flesh–and–blood enemies, but against evil rulers and authorities of the unseen world, against mighty powers in this dark world, and against evil spirits in the heavenly places.

Therefore, put on every piece of God's armor so you will be able to resist the enemy in the time of evil. Then after the battle you will still be standing firm.

Stand your ground, putting on the belt of truth and the body armor of God's righteousness. For shoes, put on the peace that comes from the Good News so that you will be fully prepared.

In addition to all of these, hold up the shield of faith to stop the fiery arrows of the devil. Put on salvation as your helmet, and take the sword of the Spirit, which is the word of God.

Ephesians 6:10–17 NLT

Lord, Your words cut me to the quick. I find it a lot easier being a part-time Sunday Christian instead of a full-time, 24/7 soldier of Christ. Send me through basic training Lord, again and again until I finally understand. Amen.

Let's think about being ready and in the mood...

1. What am I like when I'm not in the mood to be a soldier of Christ? Grouchy? Happy? Sad?

2. Am I ever in the mood to be fully God's person?
   When?

3. What can I do to become a 24/7 soldier of Christ?

4. Now?
   If not now, why not and when?

_____

_____

_____

_____

_____

_____

_____

_____

_____

_____

_____

Heaven

I have often wondered if there are dogs in Heaven. I hope so. You see, I love dogs — big gentle dogs especially, but little dogs and middle sized dogs too. In "The Sacred Diary of Adrian Plass (aged 37 ¾)" by Adrian Plass[5], I came across the following passage...

Suddenly found myself on my feet. Felt about six years old as I spoke, "I don't want to die..."

"No," said Father John, "neither do I. Life can be very good. I'm sure Jesus didn't want to die either. His friends and family, the natural world, laughter, tears, work — He loved it all I'm sure."

"But Heaven — the idea of Heaven seems so ... I don't know..."

"What is your name?" asked the monk.

"Adrian..."

"Adrian, what are you interested in — really interested in, I mean?"

"Cricket." Didn't mean to tell the truth. It just slipped out.

"So," said Father John, "for you, Adrian, God has to make sure that Heaven is at least as exciting and stimulating and satisfying as scoring a century (100 points) against Australia (cricket team) at Lords (the preeminent cricket field in Great Britain). Is that your wife sitting next to you?"

Anne smiled and nodded.

"If Adrian keels over suddenly, my dear, and he's on the point of death, you'll know what to do now?"

"Yes," laughed Anne, "I'll buckle a pair of (cricket) pads on him — quick."

Felt as if someone had opened a window and let air into a stuffy room.

If Adrian wants Heaven to be as exciting and stimulating and satisfying as a record–setting cricket match, then I want Heaven to be as fun and exciting and stimulating and satisfying as a room full of dogs — all sizes and breeds.

I strongly suspect Heaven will be very exciting. After all, Jesus made us this big promise...

There is more than enough room in my Father's home. If this were not so, would I have told you that I am going to prepare a place for you?
John 14:2 NLT

Loving Heavenly Father, I must admit that the idea of doing nothing but singing Your praises for eternity doesn't really excite me. But the idea of being in Your presence, singing Your praises, actively participating, being loved and loving other people does excite me. Help me trust Your promises for a wonderful and exciting future in Your Heaven. And Lord, if dogs are there, too, that will be great. Amen.

Let's think about heaven...

1. What do I really think Heaven will be like? For me will it be full of dogs?
2. What special activity do I hope to find there for me to do?
3. What don't I expect to find there?
4. How does this make me feel about life after death?

_____

_____

_____

_____

_____

_____

_____

_____

_____

_____

_____

_____

_____

_____

The Weaver

An English friend told me the following illustration of free will and God's grace...

It takes two people to make a beautiful tapestry. The Master Weaver faces the front or upper side of the tapestry so that he can see the picture develop. The Assistant Weaver faces the back or lower side of the tapestry and puts in the colored threads as directed by the Master Weaver.

Once in a while the Assistant Weaver makes a mistake and puts in the wrong thread. However, instead of having the incorrect thread removed, the Master Weaver changes the picture.

So it is with our free will — God has a picture in mind when He creates us. However, because we are free to do as we wish, we sometimes put in the wrong thread. God then changes His picture to make the results of our mistakes a thing of beauty.

Sometime later I realized my mother had this plaque hanging in her home...

The Weaver

My life is but a weaving
between the Lord and me.
I know not the colors
He weaveth steadily.
At times He weaveth sorrow
and I in foolish pride
Forget He sees the upper
and I the underside.

Not till the loom is silent
and the shuttle ceases to fly
Shall He unveil the canvas
and reveal the reason why
The dark threads were as needful
in the weaver's skillful hands
As the threads of gold and silver
in the pattern that He planned.

Benjamin Malachi Franklin (1882–1965)

Running With God

The Old Testament prophet, Isaiah, gave us these words of encouragement...

You will keep in perfect peace all who trust in you, all whose thoughts are fixed on you! Trust in the LORD always, for the LORD GOD is the eternal Rock.

Isaiah 26:3-4 NLT

Paul, a follower of Jesus, wrote this in a letter...

And we know that God causes everything to work together for the good of those who love God and are called according to his purpose for them.

Romans 8:28 NLT

Loving Father, help me trust that You are always in control, watching over my every step. And when things seem to go terribly wrong, help me trust in You even more, knowing that You will turn everything to good if I only love and trust You. Amen.

Let's think about trusting God...

1. What dark threads are in my life right now?
2. Am I fighting them, trying to remove them from my life?
3. Can I trust God to make them into something beautiful?
4. Can I think of any time in the past when God turned something awful into a blessing?
5. How did that make me feel later?

_____

_____

_____

_____

_____

_____

_____

_____

_____

_____

_____

_____

Anticipation

Packing for a trip can be fun.

Planning a wedding or preparing for a new baby takes months and can be a lot of fun and also a lot of work.

Organizing a family trip to the local amusement park can be fun.

My point is that I really enjoy the anticipation of an upcoming fun event.

Unfortunately, the anticipation before the event usually lasts longer than the actual event. What took days, weeks or months of joyful anticipation may only require a few short hours or days for the actual event.

Now let me consider my anticipation of Heaven.

I must admit that I do not anticipate going to Heaven in the same way that I anticipate a fun, family event.

But shouldn't I be anticipating my trip to Heaven every day? After all, Heaven will be more wonderful and more exciting than I can ever imagine. (See "Heaven" page 78)

And what about anticipating the welcome I will receive when I do arrive in Heaven? Won't that be awesome? (See "My Friend," page 51)

In contrast to other events, the anticipation of Heaven while living here on Earth is actually very short. The actual event of living in Heaven will go on forever and ever and ever.

Also, during my anticipation and preparation for Heaven, I can store all my really important personal treasures there. Treasures like the love I have for my wife, my children and their families. Treasures like the love I have of singing hymns and praise to God.

Then when I arrive in Heaven, these things will be there with me. It's kind of like packing my luggage and having it ready for immediate departure.

The anticipation of Heaven, like the anticipation of any big event, may require a lot of work to get ready. But it can be a real joy to prepare.

Today, I will do my best to live my life in joyful anticipation of Heaven knowing all my treasures will be there with me.

Jesus said this about where we should keep our treasures...

> **Don't store up treasures here on earth, where moths eat them and rust destroys them, and where thieves break in and steal. Store your treasures in heaven, where moths and rust cannot destroy, and thieves do not break in and steal. Wherever your treasure is, there the desires of your heart will also be.**
>
> Matthew 6:19–21 NLT

Dearest Father God, forgive me when I forget about the wonderful place You have prepared for me called Heaven. Help me live today and every day from now on in great joyful anticipation of the welcome You are preparing for me. Amen.

Let's think about anticipating Heaven...

1. What was the most recent event I enjoyed anticipating?
2. How long did the anticipation last?
3. How long did the event last?
4. Am I anticipating Heaven the same way as that event?
5. If I begin living every day in joyful anticipation and preparation for Heaven, how would my life change?
6. Can I do that now?
   If not now, why not and when?

_____

_____

_____

_____

_____

_____

_____

_____

_____

_____

_____

Things Change

When God sent Adam and Eve out of the Garden of Eden He told them...

...the ground is cursed because of you. All your life you will struggle to scratch a living from it. It will grow thorns and thistles for you, though you will eat of its grains. By the sweat of your brow will you have food to eat until you return to the ground from which you were made. For you were made from dust, and to dust you will return.

Genesis 3:17b–19 NLT

King David wrote these words...

You prepare a feast for me in the presence of my enemies. You honor me by anointing my head with oil. My cup overflows with blessings.

Surely your goodness and unfailing love will pursue me all the days of my life, and I will live in the house of the LORD forever.

Psalm 23:5–6 NLT

WOW! These are very different passages. Yet, both contain a promise from God about what the future holds.

The first one, in effect, says, "I never promised you a rose garden." In that case, I guess I can't very well complain too much when I don't get my rose garden.

Things Change

Then there's the second passage that describes the banquet God prepares for us. It reminds me of that great line in "Auntie Mame" by Patrick Dennis[6] when Mame says, "Live, live, live! Life is a banquet, and most poor suckers are starving to death!"

Sometimes I get so wrapped up in my misery, my loneliness, my sorrow and my poverty of spirit that I miss the banquet that God sets before me.

I recently watched a great old movie, "The Last Starfighter"[7], and was struck by the thought expressed by Otis, "Things change, always do. You'll get your chance. Only thing is, when it comes, you got to grab it with both hands, hold on tight."

Running With God

When I am deep in the ashes of despair and misery, it is really hard for me to remember that things do change — <u>always</u>. Life does not go on the same forever. And when I'm that deep in the ashes, I have to be very careful and vigilant or I may miss the change when it comes.

> Dear Lord, please help me enjoy Your world whether it is sunny or raining. Please help me enjoy and love my own life, regardless of the circumstances I am in, knowing that You are always there with me. Amen.

Let's think about life's opportunities...

1. Right now am I in a rose garden or in a patch of thistles?

2. Was there ever an opportunity I missed because I was afraid to grab onto it?

3. What in my life keeps me from grabbing onto opportunities when they come my way?

4. What are 3 things I can do to prepare to grab onto the next opportunity?

_____

_____

_____

_____

_____

_____

_____

_____

_____

_____

_____

Love! That's All

John, a disciple of Jesus, wrote this encouragement to the followers of Jesus...

Dear friends, let us continue to love one another, for love comes from God. Anyone who loves is a child of God and knows God. But anyone who does not love does not know God, for God is love.

1st John 4:7–8 NLT)

WOW! That goes right back to what Jesus said were the two greatest commandments...

Jesus replied, "'You must love the Lord your God with all your heart, all your soul, and all your mind.' This is the first and greatest commandment. A second is equally important: 'Love your neighbor as yourself.'"

Matthew 22:37–39 NLT

Later Jesus made the second commandment even stronger...

This is my commandment: Love each other in the same way I have loved you. There is no greater love than to lay down one's life for one's friends.

John 15:12–13

So why do we argue over which church or religion has the best or greatest doctrinal statement? Why do we argue endlessly over what the church and Christians should or should not be doing? If whatever we are doing is done in love then shouldn't that be enough?

Think about it. Isn't love the only true test of a Christian? As the song says, "They will know we are Christians by our love."[15]

But then you say, "My definition of love is different than yours."

And I reply, "There should only be one definition of love — God's definition."

We know what real love is because Christ gave up his life for us. And so we also ought to give up our lives for our brothers and sisters.
1st John 3:16 NLT

Jesus Himself explained how we should love others...

You have heard the law that says, "Love your neighbor" and hate your enemy. But I say, "love your enemies! Pray for those who persecute you!" In that way, you will be acting as true children of your Father in heaven. For he gives his sunlight to both the evil and the good, and he sends rain on the just and the unjust alike.

If you love only those who love you, what reward is there for that? Even corrupt tax collectors do that much. If you are kind only to your friends, how are you different from anyone else? Even pagans do that.

Matthew 5:43:47

Lord, help me put aside all bitterness, envy, jealousy, greed, hatred, small-mindedness and religiosity. Instead, help me love, simply and unselfishly, everyone with whom I come in contact. And loving them, help me act on that love, as I hope they will act on their love for me. Amen.

Let's think about loving other Christians...

1. Do I have any strong differences with others who also call themselves "Christian?"

2. Do these differences separate me from them?
How?

3. Am I following Jesus' definition of love when I deal with or talk about these other Christians?

4. If I follow Jesus' definition of love more closely, will that change my relationship with other Christians?
How?

_____

_____

_____

_____

_____

_____

_____

_____

_____

_____

Pain And Comfort

Oswald Chambers makes the point in "My Utmost For His Highest"[8] that "If you are going to be used by God, He will take you through a multitude of experiences that are not meant for you at all, they are meant to make you useful in His hands."

If I have never experienced being in trouble and being comforted by God, how can I hope to pass on God's comfort to others?

I once heard a story of a woman who lost a child under extremely tragic circumstances. Later she started a support group for parents who had gone through similar situations.

After one speaking engagement, someone approached her and said, "I wish I could speak like you do and comfort all these people."

Her reply was a question, "Are you willing to first go through the pain and suffering I have gone through?"

When pain and suffering come, I want to run away from it as fast as I can. But there is no running away — except to Jesus. Jesus has been there. Jesus will comfort me. And, later, with His comfort I may be able to comfort others.

Pain And Comfort

God is the great comforter...

He comforts us in all our troubles so that we can comfort others. When they are troubled, we will be able to give them the same comfort God has given us.
2nd Corinthians 1:4 NLT

Lord, give me the strength and faith to go through whatever may come my way. Afterwards, help me to comfort others as You comforted me. Amen.

Let's think about pain and comfort...

1. Thinking back to a time of pain and suffering, what words or acts of comfort did I receive?

2. Which ones comforted me the most? Why?

3. Since then have I met anyone going through the same or very similar situation? If so, was I able to comfort them? How?

4. Am I going through a difficult situation right now? How is it changing my outlook on helping others in a similar situation?

_____

_____

_____

_____

_____

_____

_____

_____

_____

_____

Santa Wouldn't Do That

Everyone knows Santa Claus, who he is and what he does. But have you ever stopped to think of some of the things Santa will *never* do?

Santa will *never...*

- Drive his sleigh or car too fast
- Raise his voice to a child
- Use inappropriate language or gestures
- Smoke or drink in public
- Forget that he is Santa Claus

Why?

Because Santa never knows when a child may be watching him.

As a Christian, shouldn't I always be aware that others might be watching to see how I act and behave? Just as Santa Claus could by a wrong action terribly upset a child, as a Christian I can turn others away from God by a small, unthinking word or action.

One of our sons, hiking with a friend in Nepal, asked for shelter for the night at a small Christian monastery up in the hills. They were not made to feel welcome at all. He later told me how that made him feel and it wasn't good.

A businessman I know attends church regularly with his family and practices many habits of "good" Christians. However, his terrible attitude and treatment of other business people, even *Christian* business people, makes them wonder if Christians are really any different from anyone else.

Running With God

Over the years my wife and I visited several churches where there was no feeling of hospitality or welcome. We walked in, took a bulletin and seated ourselves. When the pastor said to do so, we shook hands with people around us. We worshiped, prayed and sang hymns. At the end of the service we walked out without anyone greeting or talking to us.

Oh yes, they appeared friendly — with those they knew. In fact, several times we saw a group of greeters and ushers talking and laughing in a group while ignoring everyone else who was coming to worship.

How many times have I seen a Christian lose their temper, snub another person, walk out of a meeting in anger, say something mean–spirited. It happens but it shouldn't.

Customer Service experts tell us it takes at least seven to twelve good experiences to overcome just one bad experience. Worse, people will often share that bad experience with others.

Some time ago a local grocery store had all their employees wear a button that said, "We want to exceed your expectations." WOW! I love it when someone exceeds my expectations. What do you suppose would happen if we all worked to exceed other people's expectations of Christians?

As a businessman I often traveled, spending weekends away from home and attending a local church by myself. Several times, in different churches, I was invited home to dinner afterwards. WOW! That lifted my spirits. I made new friends and had a great home–cooked meal and a time of wonderful Christian fellowship.

Every morning it is up to each one of us, as the Apostle Paul says, to "put on all of God's armor". (See "Not In The Mood," page 74)

Can I do it? Can you do it?

NO!

We cannot do it — at least not by ourselves.

Jesus warned us to be ready...

> **So you, too, must keep watch! For you do not know the day or hour of my return.**
>
> Matthew 25:13 NLT

O God, how can You ask such a thing? Can't I just be myself today? No, of course not. I've given myself to You.

Gentle Father, transform me today into the person You want me to be so that others will see only You when they look at me. Amen.

Let's think about how a Christian should act...

1. When was the last time I didn't act as Jesus would want me to?
2. When was the last time non–Christians saw me act that way?
3. What was their reaction?
4. Do you think they told someone else about my poor behavior?
5. What specific things am I willing to do, beginning right now today, to exceed other people's expectations of Christians?

_____

_____

_____

_____

_____

_____

_____

_____

_____

_____

_____

_____

Worry or Pray?

Trust in the LORD with all your heart; do not depend on your own understanding. Seek his will in all you do, and he will show you which path to take.

Proverbs 3:5-6 NLT

This was my mother's favorite verse and has become our family motto — it is read at family weddings, funerals and, sometimes, daily.

My mother was fond of saying, "If you are going to worry, don't bother to pray. But if you are going to pray, then you don't need to worry." It could be very upsetting to hear her say that — usually in the middle of a family crisis. But I knew in my heart that she was right and later I would think about what she said.

I have often wondered if living life is like playing the game of Life, the children's board game. If it is, then I know I have absolutely no chance of winning.

But I keep reminding myself that life is not a game and that God is watching over me and directing every turn and twist in my real day–to–day life. He said I could trust Him and so I do trust Him as much as I can. Some days that's a lot, some days not so much.

After all, trusting Him is really the only chance I have.

Isn't it?

God's word is pretty explicit about worry...

**So don't worry about these things,
saying, "What will we eat? What
will we drink? What will we wear?"
These things dominate the thoughts
of unbelievers, but your heavenly
Father already knows all your
needs. Seek the Kingdom of God
above all else, and live righteously,
and he will give you everything you
need.**

Matthew 6:31–33 NLT

**Don't worry about anything;
instead, pray about everything. Tell
God what you need, and thank him
for all he has done. Then you will
experience God's peace, which
exceeds anything we can
understand. His peace will guard
your hearts and minds as you live in
Christ Jesus.**

Philippians 4:6–7 NLT

Lord, I do believe. Please take away my worry and my unbelief. Help me fully trust You — for everything, every day. Amen.

Let's think about living real life...

1. When times are tough, do I worry or pray or both or neither?
2. Why?
3. If I live my life by all the rules and do everything right, what happens at the end of the game?

_____

_____

_____

_____

_____

_____

_____

_____

_____

_____

_____

_____

_____

_____

_____

_____

A Smaller Cross

I have yet to meet a person with whom I would trade my troubles. Although my problems seem almost overwhelming at times, everyone else's problems always seem to be greater — even those people who appear to have a "blessed" life.

You know the people I mean — the people with the better homes, the more important job or the happier marriage. However if I look deep enough, often I find they had or are having problems in some way — problems that I do not want to have.

A Smaller Cross

Let me share a story I heard from a friend...

One day a man complained to God that his cross was too big and heavy. God took the man to a large fenced–in field with a small entrance gate and said, "Go inside and leave your cross by the gate. Inside you will find crosses of many different sizes and shapes. Take whichever one you like."

"Wow," the man thought, "this is more like it." Leaving his cross inside the gate, he went into the field.

Inside the fenced–in field were hundreds of crosses. And, yes, some were bigger than the others, but even the smallest one he found was much bigger than the cross he had been carrying.

After searching through all the crosses for several hours, the man headed back towards the gate in disappointment. Nearing the gate he saw off to the side a small cross. It was smaller than any other cross he had found in the entire field. Joyfully he picked it up and carried it through the gate to show it to God.

"See what I found," he cried joyfully as he approached God. "It is just the right size for me. I can carry this cross."

"I'm glad you can handle it," God replied. "That is the same cross you brought here."

Jesus said this about carrying our cross...

Then he said to the crowd, "If any of you wants to be my follower, you must turn from your selfish ways, take up your cross daily, and follow me.

Luke 9:23 NLT

Lord, forgive me when I balk and complain about the size of my cross. Help me realize that You have made my cross the perfect size to fit me that I might bear it joyfully for You. Amen.

A Smaller Cross

Let's think about my cross...

1. What size is my cross?
   Is it too big or too small for me?
2. If my cross is too big for me, what can I do about it?
3. Is my cross the same size it was 5, 10 or more years ago?
4. What size do I expect it to be in the future?
5. When I see someone struggling with their cross, how can I help?

_____

_____

_____

_____

_____

_____

_____

_____

_____

_____

_____

Shaken Or Stirred?

As I read "Irish Stew!" by Andrew Greeley[9], I came across this passage.

> Jesus had a very bad habit of refusing to fit into anyone's paradigms. He learned a lot from the Pharisees, but He wasn't one of them. He may have hung out with the Essenes, but He was not a compulsive hand–washer. He was surely a Jew, steeped in the Torah, but He put a very different spin on it.
>
> He was charming and even witty and told wonderful stories but He refused to be a celebrity. He dealt politely with those in authority, but did not sign on with them.
>
> Half the time He reassured people and the other half of the time He scared them. He told all the old stories but with new and disconcerting endings. He was patently a troublemaker. Which is why they had to get rid of Him.

It's been that way ever since. Everyone claims Him for their own, He's on our side. He's doing things our way. He confirms what we say. Then when we think we've sewed Him up, He's not there anymore.

When we have domesticated Jesus, we may have a very interesting person on our hands, even a superstar maybe. Alas, it is not the real Jesus. He's gone somewhere else, preaching His contradictions about His Father's kingdom and stirring up His kind of trouble. A Jesus who does not disconcert and shake us up is not Jesus at all.

Ouch! How many times have I gotten comfortable with Jesus? You know what I mean — just gently stirred. And then, when I think I've got everything under control and comfortable, He shakes up my life, usually pretty hard. I often say, "Life is full of surprises." That means Jesus has just shaken me up again.

It bothers me when I find a church or Sunday school or home study group or any cluster of Christians who believe they "correctly" understand Jesus.

You can spot them pretty easily when they begin saying things like "Ours is the only way to Heaven" or, "You're not worshipping the right Jesus" or, worst of all, "You must worship Jesus our way." These people really need to be shaken up.

Too often we forget the things that bind us together as Christians — love of Jesus, love of each other, faith in His resurrection, sharing the bread and wine in remembrance of Him. These things are, or should be, much stronger than the things that separate us — the days and times we worship, the exact wording of this or that creed or document, our methods of worship, our belief in various "writings" or prophets, the songs we sing, the list seems to go on and on.

Isn't it enough that I love Jesus as He reveals Himself to me today? Isn't it enough that I am willing to change as my understanding grows and as He shakes me up?

The Apostle Paul said this about how God will shake us all...

> **Be careful that you do not refuse to listen to the One who is speaking. For if the people of Israel did not escape when they refused to listen to Moses, the earthly messenger, we will certainly not escape if we reject the One who speaks to us from heaven!**

When God spoke from Mount Sinai his voice shook the earth, but now he makes another promise: "Once again I will shake not only the earth but the heavens also."

This means that all of creation will be shaken and removed, so that only unshakable things will remain.

Since we are receiving a Kingdom that is unshakable, let us be thankful and please God by worshiping him with holy fear and awe.

Hebrews 12:25–28

Lord God of Heaven and Earth, Creator of the Universe, I trustingly and fearfully ask You to shake me up. Shake me out of my complacency and my comfortableness.

Today help me see You, Your Son, Jesus, and the Holy Spirit in a new way. Help me see other believers as Your children.

Finally, do not allow me to create a stumbling block for anyone who wishes to find You. Amen.

Let's think about how I understand other Christians...

1. Do I tend to include or exclude people when I consider if they are really a Christian or not?

2. Should I be the one deciding if they are "really" Christians?

3. With people whom I exclude, are the areas where we both believe the same larger or smaller than the areas where we disagree?

4. How has my understanding of God changed over the past year, five years, ten years?

_____

_____

_____

_____

_____

_____

_____

_____

_____

_____

They Call Me Grandpa

I ring the doorbell and children open the door, all yelling, "GRANDPA!"

My doorbell rings and when I open the door there are children yelling, "GRANDPA!"

The phone rings, I pick it up and hear a child yelling, "HI GRANDPA!"

What fun!!!!!

I now have ten grandchildren and they all call me grandpa.

Grandpa!

What a wonderful name that is. It is music to my ears. I love it when they call me grandpa. It makes me feel better when I hear them call me grandpa or refer to me in a conversation as grandpa.

The only thing better is when they come running at me with arms wide open to hug me and at the same time calling "Grandpa" with a wonderful sound of joy in their voice. It makes my heart soar.

However, let's also be realistic. Being a grandpa is a huge responsibility but one I gladly take on. "What responsibility?" you ask. If I am grandpa, then I am not a parent, not a schoolteacher or a Sunday school teacher. But I am a teacher of many things. And being grandpa means I must be totally trustworthy and totally honest.

I will never lie to a grandchild. I may not tell them the entire story because it may not be appropriate, but I will never lie to them. Once, several years ago, I told a "white lie" and my oldest granddaughter caught me. It was then I realized that I could not, would not, ever tell a lie, not even a "white lie," to my grandchildren.

Consequently, my grandchildren know I will never lie to them, that they are totally safe with me, that I will never hurt them and that I will do my best to have fun with them and to let them have fun with me. I may even spoil them a little from time to time.

As I was thinking about how great being called grandpa makes me feel, I got to thinking about what we call God and Jesus and how it must make them feel.

I remember something that really struck me in Mel Gibson's movie "The Passion of the Christ"[14]. The people around Jesus called Him "Lord." But they didn't say it the way you and I might say it. We tend to say it like we're talking to royalty — a little stilted, holding Him at arm's length.

In the movie "Lord" was said with great love, tenderness and closeness. In fact, if they had used the word "Love" instead of the word "Lord," it would have sounded the same. Have you ever referred to someone close to you as "Love?" They used "Lord" the same way.

Running With God

Do you suppose Jesus likes to be called "Lord" as much as I like to be called "Grandpa?" Maybe even more? And what about all those other wonderful names the Bible tells us we can call Him? I once counted over 100 names for Jesus in the Bible.

The Old Testament is full of many wonderful names for God; here are just a few with their Hebrew version:

- Elohay Mishpat — God Of Justice (Isaiah 30:18)
- Elohay Selichot — God Of Forgiveness (Nehemiah 9:17)
- Elohay Mikarov — God Who Is Nearby (Jeremiah 23:23)
- Elohay Mauzi — God Of My Strength (Psalm 43:2)

On the other side of this discussion are two big questions.

1. How do you suppose God feels when we take His name in vain? I know that if one of my grandchildren calls me a bad name and not "Grandpa" it really hurts — a lot. Do you suppose God feels the same way when we misuse His name?

2. How do you explain God's love to a person who has been terribly hurt, maybe even molested, by a parent or grandparent? I don't know the answer to this one. If you do, please share it with me.

So what have I learned from being called grandpa?

I've learned that God wants me to run towards Him like I want my grandchildren to run towards me — with my arms wide open, totally trusting and calling Him Lord, Father, Love or one His many other wonderful names.

I don't do it as often as I know I should but when I do it's wonderful.

The Bible clearly tells us how to refer to God...

> **You must not misuse the name of the LORD your God. The LORD will not let you go unpunished if you misuse his name.**
>
> Exodus 20:7 NLT

> **Now we call him, "Abba, Father." For his Spirit joins with our spirit to affirm that we are God's children.**
>
> Romans 8:15b–16 NLT

My Father, my Love, my God, I'm beginning to understand that a wonderful relationship between a grandpa and his grandchildren is only a small taste of the relationship You want to have with me.

Come into my life today. Help me trust completely in You as I run towards You with my arms wide open in love of You. Amen.

Let's think about what we call God...

1. Do I ever misuse God's name?

2. What do I mean when I call God or Jesus "Lord?"

3. How would it make me feel towards God if I called Him "Love" or one of the other names listed in the Bible?

4. What are my favorite names for God and Jesus?
   What do those names mean to me?

_____

_____

_____

_____

_____

_____

_____

_____

_____

_____

_____

_____

_____

Thoughts On A Mountain Stream

One warm summer day, while sitting on a rock next to a rushing, bubbling mountain stream, I happened to consider a single drop of water as it moved down stream.

Occasionally during its trip to the ocean my drop of water touches a rock or a tree root or a fish or a bear catching fish or another animal drinking water or a child playing in the water. Sometimes my drop of water moves quite swiftly, sometimes it moves dreamily and sometimes it is caught in a side pool where it may grow stagnant and perhaps dry up completely.

Our lives are often like my drop of water. We often think we are too small to have any lasting effect on the world. Yet my drop of water, working together with all the other drops of water, grinds down huge boulders into fine sand or digs ditches a mile deep like the Grand Canyon.

Thoughts On A Mountain Stream

I especially like to think about the effect my drop of water has on a child playing in the water and the resulting fun they have.

Does my drop of water know how it affected everything it touched? I don't think so; and neither do we know how we affect everyone we touch. But just because we do not know how we have affected someone does not mean we did not have an effect, no matter how small, on everyone we touched.

Daily we leave a trail of "touches" behind us as we go about our business — perhaps a smile given and maybe returned, perhaps a disapproving frown, perhaps a laugh or a twinkle in our eye, perhaps a tear.

Once while in the hospital being terribly sick to my stomach, an unnamed nurse quietly handed me a clean, warm, damp washcloth to wipe my face. How wonderful it felt. I have never forgotten that simple act of kindness even though it was over 50 years ago. Her unspoken kindness has inspired me to daily try to do simple acts of kindness for others.

We all want to leave our mark on the world before we leave it — something people will have to favorably remember us. Yet, after considering my single drop of water in a mountain stream, I realize I have already touched thousands of lives — some for good, some for bad. My goal now is to make sure that every touch—in the hours, days, weeks or years I have left — is for good.

How many lives will you touch today? Will your touches be for good?

Jesus talked about "touching" the lives of others...

For I was hungry, and you fed me. I was thirsty, and you gave me a drink. I was a stranger, and you invited me into your home. I was naked, and you gave me clothing. I was sick, and you cared for me. I was in prison, and you visited me.

...when you did it to one of the least of these my brothers and sisters, you were doing it to me!
Matthew 25:35–36, 40 NLT

Lord, help me to not become so focused on my goals and my dreams and my needs that I am not aware of those around me and their goals, their dreams and their needs.

Make me always willing to share with others a smile, a laugh, a listening ear, a sympathetic heart or an encouraging word. Amen.

Thoughts On A Mountain Stream

Let's think about lives that I touched recently...

1. Let me make a list of all the lives I may have already touched yesterday and today.

2. How many people are on my list?

3. Now let me put a plus sign (+) next to each person on my list if the touch was for good, a minus sign (−) if the touch was bad or a zero (0) if the touch was neutral.

4. How many of the people on my list did I mark with a plus sign?

5. What about the people I marked with a plus? Is there anything they have in common? Can I see a pattern?

6. What about the people on my list I didn't mark with a plus? What do they have in common? Is there a pattern?

7. What could I have done to make a neutral zero (0) touch a good plus (+) touch?

_____

_____

_____

_____

_____

_____

Trials And Tribulations

If anyone was entitled to the "good" life it was Mary, the mother of Jesus. After all, she was personally selected by God to bear His only Son.

So what did she get for her trouble?

- She was shunned by her hometown people who thought she had been having sex before she got married — an offense for which, under Jewish law, she could be stoned.
- In the final stages of pregnancy she had to take a long trip of about 80 miles, walking and maybe riding on the back of a donkey.
- She had to give birth to her firstborn child in a stable without her mother or any other loving female relatives to help.
- Instead of returning home, she and her husband and newborn child had to flee for their lives to Egypt, again maybe on the back of a donkey. Did they even speak the language? I doubt it.

And that was all before her son was even out of diapers.

These trials had nothing to do with her personally. They had everything to do with her son.

As I look back on my life there were many situations where our family went through difficult circumstances. Looking back, I now understand what wonderful blessings some of these times turned out to be for our children.

In fact, the blessings were so great that I would willingly go through similar difficulties many times over for the sake of our children.

One situation developed when I was laid off and had to find a new job. I found one 100 miles away. We sold our home and moved. Five months after we moved I again lost my job. One year after we moved we finally sold our house. At the closing we had to write a check to help pay off our mortgage. A real bummer, right?

But, wait a minute. That year was a very real blessing to our family.

- Six months before we moved, our oldest son, David, went to New Zealand as an exchange student for a year. When he came home we had been moved for six months. He came home to finish his senior year of high school in a new school in a new town. He didn't know anyone. During this time he became closer to his family, especially his brother who was 20 months younger. They became best friends.

- Our second son, Paul, was in high school. Without his outgoing older brother to outshine him, Paul blossomed — making friends, playing a clarinet in the marching band at all the local football games, becoming more confident and mature.
- Our daughter, Joy, started middle school just as we moved, leaving behind a very close friend. In fact, they were like two peas in a pod. Unfortunately her friend's mother had made some very bad choices. Years later we found out that our daughter's friend had been in drug rehab several times. I know that if we had not moved out of town, our daughter would have very likely followed her friend into making bad choices.

When we left that town after living there a year, our family was much stronger. We had seen God working in our lives.

So next time you are having troubles, be patient, trust God and He will bring you through with blessings.

From the Apostle Paul we have a rock solid verse to rely on...

And we know that God causes everything to work together for the good of those who love God and are called according to his purpose for them.

Romans 8:28 NLT

Lord, help me have faith in Your love during the bad times as well the good times, knowing that You are always totally in control. Amen.

Running With God

Let's think about hard times...

1. What events in my life were difficult at the time but later I saw a blessing come from them?

2. Were the blessings for me or for someone else?

3. What have I learned from these events?

_____

_____

_____

_____

_____

_____

_____

_____

_____

_____

_____

_____

_____

_____

_____

_____

Choices

Several years ago "What Would Jesus Do?" was a popular phrase among many Christians. Some people even wore bracelets and t–shirts with "WWJD" on them.

However, I prefer what Moses told the Israelites so many years ago when they were wandering in the wilderness after leaving Egypt...

> **Today I have given you the choice between life and death, between blessings and curses. Now I call on Heaven and earth to witness the choice you make. Oh, that you would *choose life*, so that you and your descendants might live!**
> Deuteronomy 30:19–20 NLT

Choose Life!

I like that short phrase because it includes everything that Jesus would do and more...

- When I am tempted to say something negative or mean–spirited, "Choose Life" helps me either to keep quiet or to say something positive.
- When I am tempted to criticize instead of giving love and support, "Choose Life" helps me to change my attitude.
- When I am discouraged and depressed, "Choose Life" helps me take action to move on to a more positive outlook.
- When I am tempted by sin, "Choose Life" helps me to move away from that sin.

Dear Lord, please help me at every time and in every situation choose life and not death. In choosing life, help me love Your people, whether they are loveable or unlovable.

Finally, please help me love my own life, regardless of the circumstances I am in, knowing that You are always there with me. Amen.

Let's think about choosing life...

1. Can I think of someone in the Bible who made a bad decision — chose death?

2. What was the situation they were in and why did they make that choice?

3. Can I think of someone in the Bible who made a good decision — chose life?

4. What was the situation they were in and why did they make that choice?

5. Can I think of a time when I made a good or bad decision — decided to choose or not choose life?
   What were the results?

6. Would adopting the phrase "Choose Life" as my personal motto require any changes in my life?
   Can I start today?
   If no, why not and when?

_____

_____

_____

_____

_____

_____

_____

In Bondage To Sin

...all have sinned and fall short of the glory of God.

Romans 3:23

In many worship services part of the prayers or liturgy include a confession of our sins. In some denominations the pastor then reminds us that God forgives us our sins.

But forgiveness alone is not enough.

If I am in bondage to sin, I also need freedom from my slavery to sin. Otherwise, as a slave to the sin I will continue to sin. Where do I find that release from this slavery?

The Apostle Paul asked the same question. Thank God, he also found the answer.

The trouble is with me, for I am all too human, a slave to sin. I don't really understand myself, for I want to do what is right, but I don't do it. Instead, I do what I hate.

But if I know that what I am doing is wrong, this shows that I agree that the law is good. So I am not the one doing wrong; it is sin living in me that does it.

And I know that nothing good lives in me, that is, in my sinful nature. I want to do what is right, but I can't. I want to do what is good, but I don't. I don't want to do what is wrong, but I do it anyway.

But if I do what I don't want to do, I am not really the one doing wrong; it is sin living in me that does it.

I have discovered this principle of life — that when I want to do what is right, I inevitably do what is wrong.

I love God's law with all my heart. But there is another power within me that is at war with my mind. This power makes me a slave to the sin that is still within me.

Oh, what a miserable person I am! Who will free me from this life that is dominated by sin and death?

Thank God! The answer is in Jesus Christ our Lord. So you see how it is: In my mind I really want to obey God's law, but because of my sinful nature I am a slave to sin.

So now there is no condemnation for those who belong to Christ Jesus. And because you belong to him, the power of the life–giving Spirit has freed you from the power of sin that leads to death.

The law of Moses was unable to save us because of the weakness of our sinful nature. So God did what the law could not do.

He sent his own Son in a body like the bodies we sinners have. And in that body God declared an end to sin's control over us by giving his Son as a sacrifice for our sins.
Romans 7:14b–8:3 NLT

Most merciful God, I confess that I am in bondage to sin and cannot free myself. I have sinned against You in thought, word, and deed, by what I have done and by what I have left undone.

I have not loved You with my whole heart; I have not loved my neighbors as myself.

For the sake of Your Son, Jesus Christ, have mercy on me. Forgive me, renew me, and lead me, so that I may delight in Your will and walk in Your ways, to the glory of Your holy name. Amen.

Paraphrased from The Confiteor, Part of the introduction of the Mass, Approximately 1100 AD

Let's think about bondage to sin...

First read the two primary commandments (Matthew 22:37–40) and the complete 10 commandments (Exodus 20:1–17).

1. Am I in bondage to sin?

2. Sin affects everyone it touches, not just the sinner. Who else is my sin touching?

3. Do I really want to give up my sin? After all, sometimes sin can be fun.

4. If I don't really want to give it up, am I at least willing to ask God to be made willing? Okay, I'll do it now...

> *Most merciful God, I am in sin and, I confess, deep in my heart I really don't want to give it up. But, trusting in Your love and mercy, I am now willing for You to make me willing to give it up. Please help me. Amen.*

_____

_____

_____

_____

_____

Made In God's Image

So God created human beings in his own image. In the image of God he created them; male and female he created them.

Genesis 1:27 NLT

I really like that verse. It says that God doesn't make junk!

Period!

This chapter is not easy for me to write, to share my feelings and thoughts openly, to expose myself this way. However, I was encouraged by others to open myself up more, to put more of *me* into my writings. So for what it is worth, here I go.

Several years ago it was suggested that I might have Asperger's syndrome. Asperger's is part of the autism spectrum.

In early 2011 I visited a Neurologist who diagnosed me with Tourette's syndrome because of my mostly uncontrollable facial tics. I've had them since I was five years old. Tourette's is on the autism spectrum.

Reading books on Asperger's has helped me a lot. I finally realized why all my life I've felt like a very square peg that didn't want to and couldn't fit into the round hole.

It is not my purpose to document here all the symptoms, difficulties and advantages of Asperger's syndrome or autism. But I will highlight a few that apply to me.

Temple Grandin's book, "Thinking In Pictures"[10], helped me realize that somewhat like her, I have "movie strips" going through my mind much of the time.

These "movie strips" can bring on post—traumatic stress as I unwillingly replay unpleasant events from any time in my life. Even worse, the slightest prospect of an upcoming unpleasant event can trigger pre—traumatic stress as I watch "movies" of how the event may play out — usually showing the worst possible outcome. And the "movie" may play over and over and over.

In addition, I cannot accurately "read" people's facial expressions, voice tones and body language. Consequently I am usually completely surprised and caught off guard when someone expresses their displeasure with me. This is usually followed by my giving a sincere apology for what I said or did or by my finding a new job.

This has happened more times than I can count and I do not like it at all. Each time this happens I have a very real, very strong physical reaction like receiving a very hard "sucker punch" to the stomach. And it creates one more unpleasant "movie" to add to the growing library of horror films stored in my mind.

However, I have found that there are some advantages and blessings. I can fully concentrate on a task and stick to it until it is finished, skipping meals, sleep and anything else to get it done. This is very helpful when I have a project like writing this book, creating a web site or designing a spreadsheet. By the way, I dream about spreadsheets. I love them.

Also, I see patterns in events that seem obvious to me but other people don't see. I believe it is this gift that has helped me be aware of the "nudges from God" that are the foundation of this book.

A year or so ago I was present when an award–winning essay was read aloud. In it the Christian author spoke of how when Jesus comes again then all will be perfect in the world. He went on to say this included Jesus healing his brother who has Down syndrome so his brother would be then perfect.

I almost walked out in disgust because, well, let me share with you a story. This is from Morris West's book, "The Clowns of God"[11], in which the returned Jesus Christ talks about a girl with Down syndrome.

> **I know what you are thinking. You need a sign. What better one could I give but to make this little one whole and new? I could do it; but I will not.**

> I am the Lord and not a conjurer. I gave this mite a gift I denied to all of you — eternal innocence. To you she looks imperfect — but to me she is flawless, like the bud that dies unopened or the fledgling that falls from the nest to be devoured by ants.
>
> She will never offend me, as all of you have done. She will never pervert or destroy the work of my Father's hands. She is necessary to you.

A person with Down syndrome is not *damaged goods*.

And **neither am I and neither are you!**.

God has made each one of us in ***His Image!*** There are no mistakes in God's Kingdom.

So, yes, I sometimes, well actually quite often, frustrate and upset my family because of what I do or say or how I do it or how I say it. I'm truly sorry they are upset but that is who I am.

And who I am is one of God's children, loved and forgiven by the Creator of the Universe.

Jesus Christ died on the cross for ME!

And for you!

What more does anyone need to know before they accept me or you for who we are, as we are?

Creator of the universe, you created me in your image. That is awesome. Give me the strength and courage to go out into Your world proudly because I know I am one of Your children.

Most of all, help me to treat all others with respect, kindness and love because You created them. Amen.

Let's think about how God created me...

While these questions may seem too personal to be answered and discussed in a group, I encourage you to do so. Find a group of close friends and share with each other using lots of love, laughter and prayer.

1. How am I different than anyone else I know?

2. What problems do my differences cause for me?

3. How do I feel when others comment on my differences?

4. What problems do my differences cause for others?

5. How is the world better because of how God made me?

6. How do I react to people with obvious differences — like autism, Down syndrome, seriously overweight, a stutter or other handicap?

7. Why do I think God made me the way I am?

_____

_____

_____

_____

_____

Running With God

What's Next For Me?

Should I take this new job?

Does God approve?

Should I marry this person?

What does God want of me?

How many times have I asked questions like these? Every Christian I know struggles with these kinds of questions.

As I understand the Bible, God first gives us a desire to serve Him in a specific way. Then He provides the answer to that desire so that we can then give Him our thanks and praise.

Neat!

God doesn't want me to do something I am unsuited to do. He doesn't want me to do something that will make me miserable.

He does want me to do something that will honor Him and further His kingdom here on Earth.

The theologian Frederick Buechner said in his book "Wishful Thinking: A Seeker's ABC"[13], "There are all different kinds of voices calling you to all different kinds of work... (and) the place God calls you to is the place where your deep gladness and the world's deep hunger meet."

There are times in my life when I have no clue what I want to do or what God might want me to do. So I try to wait on the Lord. I'm not very good at that.

We often forget that the Apostle Paul waited three years after his encounter on the road with Jesus before God directed him what to do.

Running With God

During my waiting time I pray, I read, I talk to friends and family. And then, eventually, I usually know what I should do.

Such was the case with writing this book. I have thought about it for over ten years. This past spring I found myself at a time in my life when I didn't know what to do with myself. I needed to move forward but I didn't know which way to go. Nothing was clear.

So I prayed. I discussed my situation with friends and family. I waited. I had a shoulder operation to fix a torn rotator cuff. I had fun with my family. I prayed. I waited.

Then one day, after about three months, I found myself at my computer working on this book.

So what's next?

I have no idea.

But I do know it will be a challenge; it might be fun, or not, and that God will be holding my hand the whole time.

In the Bible God promises to guide us to what pleases Him...

> **Take delight in the LORD, and he will give you your heart's desires.**
> Psalms 37:4 NLT

> **For God is working in you, giving you the desire and the power to do what pleases him.**
> Philippians 2:13 NLT

Dear God in Heaven, help me recognize the desires You have placed in my heart. Help me run forward in faith, acting on those desires, knowing You are always right there beside me, holding my hand, every step of the way. Lord, let all I do and say bring honor and glory to Your name. Amen

Running With God

Let's think about what's next...

1. Am I uncertain of what I should be doing with my life?

2. Am I in a rush to just do something, anything, or am I quietly waiting on the Lord?

3. Have I ever rushed to do something without waiting for direction from God? How did it work out?

4. If I don't know what to do, can I use this time to help others, improve myself and draw closer to God?

5. Let me make a list of what I can do right now.
   Can I start now?
   If not, why not and when?

_____

_____

_____

_____

_____

_____

_____

_____

_____

_____

What's Next For You?

I was baptized as an infant and raised in a Presbyterian Church. It was there I learned to love the hymns and even to love God. But I always felt something was lacking. The relationship I had with God just didn't seem to be enough. I struggled with this a lot while I was growing up — praying hard, trying to be a better person (and always failing). I didn't know what to do.

In 1976 my wife and I and our three small children moved to a small town west of London, England (see "Running With God," page 3). Up to this point I had always considered myself something of a problem solver like the hero in the 1950's TV series "Have Gun — Will Travel". But once in England, experiencing new situations, working in France, Holland and Germany, I wasn't so sure of myself.

My faith in God was being stretched. I felt as if I were on the edge of a giant chasm with a huge 5 foot diameter rope across it. The rope represented giving my life to Jesus. My mind told me the rope would never break and that I wouldn't fall but my heart wasn't so sure. I felt I either had to get on the rope and cross the chasm or turn around and walk away forever.

Running With God

During this time we had started attending a small Baptist church across the road from our home. One evening a visiting lay preacher (a Presbyterian lawyer from Clover, South Carolina) came to our home and explained how Jesus wants to have a *personal* relationship with each of us. My friend talked to me about placing my **full** trust in God — for everything.

He shared with me some verses and prayed with me — verses and a prayer similar to what I'll share with you in a moment. We knelt together in our living room and we prayed and I gave my life to God.

Several days later I felt a strong need to be baptized again and was baptized by immersion in the Baptist Church in Henley–On–Thames, England.

In the years since then I have been learning to run with God and I'm still learning — every day. It hasn't always been easy as you have learned from some of my stories. But God has *always* been there — faithful, forgiving, trustworthy and loving.

So how about you? Are you already running with God? If so, HALLELUJAH!

If not, are you now ready to begin trusting God? Are you ready to be adopted by Him as one of His children as I was?

Earlier in this chapter I described how I came to commit my life to Jesus. However, that is not the only way it happens.

What's Next For You?

My parents both loved Jesus very much and were completely committed to Him. However, their process of commitment took much longer — I'm guessing it was 10 years at least. As a child growing up I saw that each year they became more and more committed to Jesus until by the time I was an adult they were fully committed to Him.

Did they go through a "4–Step" program? No. Did they get re–baptized? No. Did they understand the question, "Are you saved?" No.

Did they understand they were sinners and that Jesus died for them? YES!!! Did they have a close, daily, personal relationship with Jesus? YES!!!

You see, Jesus makes Himself known to each one of us in a unique and special way. Some people can point to a specific date and time they made a commitment to Jesus. For others it is a growing process over a period of time.

Is one way better than another? No!

If you are ready to make a commitment right now, then don't delay. As my pastor says, "Don't make a commitment until you are ready but don't delay one second more."

A word of warning:

Giving your life to Jesus, accepting His gifts of forgiveness and eternal life that He offers, is NOT the path to an easy life. On the contrary, as a follower of Jesus your life may become even more difficult than it is now. But like me, you will soon find the joy builds up inside you and carries you through life's trials.

You see, God promises that we need never fear and that He will always be with us...

> **Don't be afraid, for I am with you.**
> **Don't be discouraged, for I am your**
> **God. I will strengthen you and help**
> **you. I will hold you up with my**
> **victorious right hand.**
>
> Isaiah 41:10 NLT

Here is what you need to understand and believe...

No one is perfect — there are no exceptions. None of us can meet God's holy standards.

> **For everyone has sinned; we all fall**
> **short of God's glorious standard.**
>
> Romans 3:23 NLT

As sinners we all deserve death.

> **For the wages of sin is death, but**
> **the free gift of God is eternal life**
> **through Christ Jesus our Lord.**
>
> Romans 6:23 NLT

What's Next For You?

As the Apostle Paul said, God has already paid the price for our sins. Jesus died in our place in order to give us life.

But God showed his great love for us by sending Christ to die for us while we were still sinners.

Romans 5:8 NLT

Jesus is the *only* way out of sin and death. He said...

I am the way, the truth, and the life. No one can come to the Father except through me.

John 14:6 NLT

When you understand and believe these things, then salvation is as simple as A – B – C...

A – **Admit** to yourself and to God that you are a sinner

B – **Believe** in your heart that Jesus died and rose from the dead. Believing in Jesus is not just acknowledging that the events really happened. Believing in Jesus is **trusting** in His dying as a substitute for you and His resurrection for **your** salvation.

C – **Confess** (tell others) that God raised Jesus from the dead and that you accept Jesus Christ as the Lord of your life.

Now ask God to speak to your heart and begin to trust Christ from your heart. Pray something like this...

Lord God, I know that I have broken Your laws and that I am a great sinner. I am truly sorry for everything I have done wrong. Please forgive me and help keep me from sinning again.

I do believe that Your Son, Jesus Christ, died on a cross for my sins, was resurrected from the dead, is alive and hears my prayers.

Jesus, I do want You to be Lord of my life, to rule and reign in my heart from this day forward.

Please send Your Holy Spirit to help me love, trust and follow You, wherever You may lead me for the rest of my life. Amen.

What's Next For You?

Know in your heart that you are now assured of salvation and eternal life.

Jesus said...

For God loved the world so much that he gave his one and only Son, so that everyone who believes in him will not perish but have eternal life.

God sent his Son into the world not to judge the world, but to save the world through him.
John 3:16–17 NLT

And anyone who believes in God's Son has eternal life. Anyone who doesn't obey the Son will never experience eternal life but remains under God's angry judgment.
John 3:36 NLT

The next step is for you to talk with God (pray) and ask Him for guidance and direction. Ask Him to send you a Christian whom you can trust and who will teach you and mentor you in your walk with Christ.

If you are already attending a church, share with the pastor your new faith and trust in Christ. Ask the pastor to guide you on your new journey with Jesus.

Running With God

If you aren't attending a church or don't feel your present church can help you, you may have a relative, co–worker or a friend who is a committed Christian. Talk with them. Ask them to tell you about their relationship with God. Ask them to pray with you and for you.

Ask them to take you to church with them one Sunday soon. (It's always better to go with someone than alone.) Afterwards have a meal together and talk about what you heard and saw at their church. Find out what their church believes and practices, including baptism and Holy Communion.

Look for a church that places a high value on the Bible, the Word of God. The Bible should be quoted during sermons and should be an integral part of church activities (worship, Sunday school, small groups, prayer meetings, etc.).

Look for a church that prays — prayers during worship, prayers at meetings, prayers in small groups, prayers by the pastor and prayers by the people. Look for a church that celebrates Holy Communion at least once a month.

Look for a church that offers ways for you to use your unique gifts, talents and abilities to serve God and His people. Look for a church that "reaches out" by meeting the physical, emotional, and spiritual needs of people outside the church — in your own community and in foreign countries.

What's Next For You?

Seriously consider being baptized by immersion, even if you were "sprinkled" as an infant so that you join with Jesus in His death and resurrection.

> **Or have you forgotten that when we were joined with Christ Jesus in baptism, we joined him in his death? For we died and were buried with Christ by baptism. And just as Christ was raised from the dead by the glorious power of the Father, now we also may live new lives.**
> Romans 6:3–4

Editorial Note: Just about all churches believe in baptism but they vary greatly on the details and the importance they put on it...

1) Some churches believe you *MUST* be baptized by immersion and only after you are old enough to understand what you are doing
2) Some churches believe you can be baptized either by immersion or sprinkling, either as a child or as an adult
3) Some churches really don't care how or when as long as you are baptized

I'm not going to get into a theological discussion about any of these viewpoints. I personally believe that baptism as an adult by immersion is my best and only response to what God has done for me by sending His Son to die for my sins.

If you believe differently, I will not argue with you about it. But I will continue to love you. (See "Love! That's All," page 94)

Running With God

Begin reading the Bible. There are many translations and paraphrased versions. For now pick any Bible you have access to so that you can quickly get started. Try reading your Bible while eating breakfast, lunch or dinner, first thing when you get up in the morning or the last thing before you go to bed at night.

Later as you become more knowledgeable you may wish to switch to a different version. If you have a choice, try either the New Living Translation (all the Bible quotes in this book are from there) or the New International Version.

Start your reading with one of the four Gospels — Matthew, Mark, Luke or John. Then read Acts and keep on going. For a change of pace, read Psalms and notice how King David struggled with his faith just as you and I.

By the way, it is okay to skip through some of the books of the Bible for now. Ask God and He will direct your reading.

Last, but most important, talk with God. Often! There is no set formula of words to say or time or physical position or location for prayer.

Start each day by thanking God for the new day and asking Him to run with you through everything that happens. Close each day by thanking God for running with you through the day. Continue to talk with God whenever and wherever you can.

I like to pray when I'm alone in the car. I ask Him to help me set my priorities for which tasks I should work on today — and He does.

What's Next For You?

When you pray, talk with God about the big things happening in your life, talk with Him about the small things and everything in between. There is nothing too small or too big to talk over with God. A friend of mine asks God to help him find a good parking spot for his handicapped wife.

In conclusion, please remember:
God loves you more than you can possibly imagine.

Running With God

Let's think about how I run with God...

1. When I first began reading this book, what did I think of God?

2. What do I think of God now?

3. Has my faith and trust in God grown as I read this book? If so, how?

4. If I haven't already given my life to God, am I ready to do so now?

5. If not now, why not and what must happen before I am ready?

_____

_____

_____

_____

_____

_____

_____

_____

_____

_____

_____

_____

About The Author

I live in Colorado with my wife whom I married in 1963. Our three children and their families live nearby. We have 10 grandchildren and one dog.

I am "semi–retired," spending my time with the grandchildren, writing, reading, working on my computer and doing some public speaking on both inspirational and business topics.

For the past 13 years I have also been Santa Claus. In 2011 over 6,000 children will sit on my lap and tell me what they want for Christmas. Once in a while I become Saint Nicholas and explain how Jesus *IS* the real reason for the season.

For more information about my writings, my possible participation in your event or to watch videos of my speaking, please visit my web site at www.JohnTheStoryteller.com.

If you would like to comment on this book, please join me on Facebook or Amazon.com — just search for "Running With God".

In 2012 I plan to start an online blog. Look for the link at www.JohnTheStoryteller.com.

Additional copies of my books may be purchased from Amazon.com and other online retailers. For bulk copies or to sell this book at your church, please contact me directly to discuss special pricing.

Thank you for reading my book. I pray it was a blessing to you.

John M. Chilson
Longmont, CO
November 2011

Bible Verses

1st Corinthians 13:12 27
1st John 3:16 95
1st John 3:18 52
1st John 4:7–8 94
1st Peter 3:15b NLT 74
2nd Corinthians 1:4 99
2nd Kings 5:10 16
2nd Timothy 4:2a 74
Acts 4:32 39
Colossians 3:23–24 72
Deuteronomy 30:19–20 133
Deuteronomy 4:7b 55
Ephesians 6:10–17 76
Exodus 20:17 49
Exodus 20:7 121
Genesis 1:27 140
Genesis 3:17b–19 90
Hebrews 11:1 44
Hebrews 12:25–28 115
Isaiah 26:3–4 84
Isaiah 30:18 120
Isaiah 40:28–31 64
Isaiah 41:10 154
James 1:2–4 23
James 2:14–20 45
Jeremiah 23:23 120
Jeremiah 29:11 64
John 1:12–13 55
John 14:1 23
John 14:2 80
John 14:6 NLT 155
John 15:12–13 94
John 15:12–21 36
John 3:16 58

Bible Verses

John 3:16–17 NLT................................157
John 3:36 157
Luke 12:35–36 4
Luke 17:9–10.....................................72
Luke 3:11 39
Luke 9:23 110
Matthew 22:37–39.................................94
Matthew 25:13 103
Matthew 25:35–36, 40 126
Matthew 25:37–40 9
Matthew 5:43:47 96
Matthew 6:19–21 87
Matthew 6:31–33 106
Nehemiah 9:17 120
Philippians 2:13 148
Philippians 2:14–15a.............................19
Philippians 4:6–7................................106
Proverbs 3:24–26 31
Proverbs 3:5–6...............................31, 105
Psalm 23:5–6 90
Psalm 34:1 68
Psalm 34:6 68
Psalm 43:2 120
Psalms 37:4 148
Romans 14:17–18 19
Romans 3:23 ....136, 154
Romans 5:8 ....59, 155
Romans 6:23 154
Romans 6:3–4.....................................159
Romans 7:14b–8:3 138
Romans 8:14–16 13
Romans 8:15b–16 121
Romans 8:28.................................84, 131
Romans 8:35–39 69
Romans 9:20b–21...................................8

Sources

The sources in bold are my personal recommendations. Enjoy.

1 "Have Thine Own Way, Lord," lyrics by Adelaide A. Pollard and music by George C. Stebbins (1907), quoted in "A Dangerous Song" on page 7

2 "Luther's German Bible" by Martin Luther (1522), an excerpt from "An Introduction to St. Paul's Letter to the Romans," quoted in "What Is Faith?" on page 41

3 "Lord Of The Dance," song by Sydney Carter (1967), quoted in "Sing Hallelujah On Good Friday?" on page 67

4 "Dune" by Frank Herbert, published by Chilton Book Company (1965), quoted in "Not In The Mood" on page 74

5 **"The Sacred Diary of Adrian Plass, Aged 37–¾" by Adrian Plass, published by Zondervan (2005), quoted in "Heaven" on page 78** (A delightful book about relating to God.)

6 "Auntie Mame" by Patrick Dennis, published by Broadway (1955), quoted in "Things Change" on page 90

7 "The Last Starfighter" released in 1984, staring Lance Guest, Robert Preston and Dan O'Herlihy, quoted in "Things Change" on page 90

8 **"My Utmost for His Highest" by Oswald Chambers, published by Discovery House Publishers (1935), quoted in "Pain And Comfort" on page 98**

Sources

9 "Irish Stew!" by Andrew Greeley, published by Forge Books (2003), quoted in "Shaken Or Stirred?" on page 112

10 "Thinking In Pictures" by Temple Grandin, published by Bloomsbury (2006), mentioned in "Made In God's Image" on page 140

11 "The Clowns of God" by Morris West, published by William Morrow & Company (1981), quoted in "Made In God's Image" on page 140

12 "Attitude" quote from Charles Swindoll, author, pastor, speaker, founder of Insight For Living, www.insight.org, quote found at www.iwise.com /SVeFq, quoted in "What's My Attitude?" on page 18

13 "Wishful Thinking: A Seeker's ABC" by Frederick Buechner, published by HarperOne (1900), quoted in "What's Next For Me?" on page 147

14 "The Passion of the Christ", released in 2004, Directed by Mel Gibson, quoted in "They Call Me Grandpa" on page 118

15 "They'll Know We Are Christians By Our Love", written by Peter Scholtes with additional words and music by Carolyn Arends, published by F.E.L. Publications Ltd. (1966), quoted in "Love! That's All" on page 94

"The Holy Bible: New Living Translation, Second Edition," published by Tyndale Press (2004), Referred to throughout this book as "NLT"
Note: All quoted Bible verses use the capitalization in the New Living Translation.

Made in the USA
Middletown, DE
04 November 2022

14086250R00099